Stanton Coit

Neighbourhood Guilds

An Instrument of Social Reform. Second Edition

Stanton Coit

Neighbourhood Guilds
An Instrument of Social Reform. Second Edition

ISBN/EAN: 9783337296209

Printed in Europe, USA, Canada, Australia, Japan

Cover: Foto ©Suzi / pixelio.de

More available books at **www.hansebooks.com**

NEIGHBOURHOOD GUILDS

Crown 8vo.   Price 4s 6d.

INTRODUCTION TO THE STUDY OF ETHICS.

Adapted from the German of G. Von Gizycki,
Professor of Philosophy in the University of Berlin.

BY

STANTON COIT, Ph.D.

OPINIONS OF THE PRESS.

"May be safely recommended for the class room."—*St. James's Gazette.*

"Admirably arranged. A book which will stimulate thought."—*Spectator.*

"This is a thoroughly practical and commonsense work on morals. Dr. Coit has done a serviceable work in rendering it accessible to English readers."—*Journal of Education.*

"The German original of this book has found the best possible translator in Dr. Coit, who stands in special relation and sympathy with the author."—*Mind.*

"We can warmly praise in this book the high moral tone, the insistence on the reality and independence of the moral sentiment, the demonstration that man is not shown to pursue his selfish interest by showing that pain and pleasure are the prices that everywhere set him in motion."—*Athenæum.*

NEIGHBOURHOOD GUILDS

An Instrument of Social Reform

BY

STANTON COIT, Ph.D.

Lecturer of the South Place Ethical Society, London.

SECOND   EDITION.

London
SWAN SONNENSCHEIN & CO.
PATERNOSTER SQUARE
1892

CONTENTS.

	PAGE
I.—NEIGHBOURHOOD GUILDS AND THE INDUSTRIAL PROBLEM	1
II.—THE NEIGHBOURHOOD GUILD DEFINED—ITS CREDENTIALS	7
III.—LOCALITY IN CITIES AS A FACTOR IN REFORM —ILLUSTRATED IN RELIEF WORK	17
IV.—CO-OPERATION WITH OTHER REFORM AGENCIES	28
V.—NEUTRALITY IN RELIGION	36
VI.—ENTHUSIASM FOR THE GUILD	40
VII.—THE FAMILY AS THE MORAL UNIT OF SOCIETY	46
VIII.—SOCIAL MEETINGS FOR YOUNG MEN AND YOUNG WOMEN	52
IX.—THE DIVISION OF A GUILD INTO CLUBS	55
X.—THE SPACE NEEDED FOR ONE GUILD	60
XI.—THE LIMIT OF MEMBERSHIP IN ONE CLUB	63
XII.—A RADIATION OF GUILDS FROM A CENTRE	68
XIII.—A BODY OF TRAINED WORKERS ON SECULAR LINES	71
XIV.—THE GUILD BUDGET	78
XV.—THE TRANSFORMATION OF VARIOUS INSTITUTIONS INTO NEIGHBOURHOOD GUILDS	81

	PAGE
XVI.—THE WAY TO START A NEW GUILD . .	91
XVII.—REFORM WORK—CLASS WORK	99
XVIII.—ENTERTAINMENTS	108
XIX.—THE PERSONALITY OF THE LEADERS OF A GUILD	117
XX.—MORAL AND CIVIC INSTRUCTION IN THE GUILD	126
XXI.—THE MORAL DISCIPLINE OF THE GUILD . .	135
XXII.—WHAT CLASSES OF PEOPLE THE GUILD MAY REACH	138
XXIII.—NOT A MERE DROP IN THE OCEAN . .	147

NEIGHBOURHOOD GUILDS:

An Instrument of Social Reform.

I.

NEIGHBOURHOOD GUILDS AND THE INDUSTRIAL PROBLEM.

No one has as yet accepted, in the full sense in which he meant it, General Booth's challenge to bring forward a better scheme than his for lifting the fallen classes of society into independence and prosperity. He demanded that over against the Salvation Army and the network of measures he had proposed, any one who refused to support him should not only point out other and better methods, but also another body of workers who were ready and competent to execute them. This no one of his opponents has done.

It is true that some clergymen have announced that the Church is the proper organisation to execute Mr. Booth's suggestions, but they have said nothing to show that the Church will in any likelihood adopt the enterprise. In a similar manner the socialists insist that such a work should not be left in the hands of the Salvation Army; but they have not been able to point to any County Council or other local authority willing and able to carry out the scheme. Others, by fair and telling criticism, have shown up gross and dangerous defects, both in some important details and in the fundamental conception of Mr. Booth's plan. While such critics have been chiefly negative and destructive in intention, there is, nevertheless, visible in the background of their arguments the outline of a counter-scheme. But they, too, fail to tell us who will apply their better method. The Secretary of the Charity Organisation Society cannot say, "I will supply an adequate corps of enthusiastic workers, ready to put into practice the principles of reform I have laid down." And Mr. Bosanquet, in his admirable criticism* of Mr. Booth's scheme, does not try to con-

* "'In Darkest England' on the Wrong Track." By B. Bosanquet, M.A. London: Swan Sonnenschein & Co.

ceal his disappointment that the Salvation Army, which might have led out the unhappy denizens from Darkest England, has been set on the wrong track by its "General." But the Army having failed him, Mr. Bosanquet leaves us without a hint of where to turn for rescue.

The Neighbourhood Guild does, I believe, solve the difficulty of getting the right men as well as the right measures. If it can do this, it deserves public attention. And that large class in the community who for religious or economic reasons have found themselves unable to sanction General Booth's scheme may be glad to support another already successfully begun, which contains none of those elements of social danger felt to be inherent in the Salvation Army enterprise.

In the following pages the Neighbourhood Guild will be considered primarily as a scheme for getting the right men; only incidentally will the problem as to the right ultimate measures of industrial reform be dealt with. The former is the more pressing question of the hour. Were an adequate number of men systematically at work, attempting to understand and solve our agrarian and industrial difficulties, the just solution would be sure to dawn gradually upon the popular consciousness, and the new order be ushered in as noiselessly as the day. Whatever be the nature of the fundamental changes ultimately to be made in land-tenure, in taxation, and in the private ownership of the instruments of production, there must be a preliminary enlightenment of the great mass of the people in economic and social principles and aims, and a corresponding enthusiasm or disposition to bring about a juster order of life. But this enlightenment and the disposition to carry out specific radical reforms can only be brought about when the intellectual life of the people has been organised. The first step in social reform, if my psychology be correct, must be the conscious organisation of the intellectual and moral life of the people for the total improvement of the human lot. Out of a comprehensive aspiration issue particular resolutions to reform life on definite lines by specific means. This is true of masses of men as well as of individuals. The organisation of the intellectual and moral life of the people is the crying need of our day. Because of the lack of it, our ideals and schemes are cold, abstract, bloodless things, or, at best, are impotent; they are like spirits without bodies, they cannot make themselves seen or felt or heard; they have no hands, nor feet, nor eyes, nor tongue. Were they the true deliverers, they would be utterly powerless, handicapped by lack of tangible substance—lack of hosts of men inspired by them. If this first step, the organisation of the masses mentally and morally, were taken, the second step, the enlightenment of the people in social principles, could be easily made, and then the realization of the just state would not be remote, nor would it be brought in with violence. Now such a general organisation of the life of the people, and such a general civic instruction, are the special field of action which the Neighbourhood Guild would presume to assign to itself. How it could meet the requirements of the case, what its own internal principles and methods are, I shall attempt in these pages to point out. To do this it is not necessary for the writer to make any confession of faith as to the nationalization of land and capital. As to special measures, I shall simply assume that, whatever be the final and widest-sweeping reforms,—whether the wage system is simply to be modified or is to be superseded by a better method of production and distribution,—still the immediate line of advance will be through the organisation of all labourers, women as well as men, into trades unions, through a reduction of the hours of work, through friendly societies, through greater domestic conveniences and healthier surroundings, through better education in general, and through increased recreation and higher amusements. With these specific schemes of reform the Neighbourhood Guild is already allied. Presupposing their value and anticipating still more radical reforms, which for our present purpose may remain undefined as the secret of the future, I turn to consider the internal principles of the Neighbourhood Guild and its methods of work.

II.
THE NEIGHBOURHOOD GUILD DEFINED—ITS CREDENTIALS.

THE very name, Neighbourhood Guild, suggests the fundamental idea which this new institution embodies: namely, that, irrespective of religious belief or non-belief, all the people, men, women, and children, in any one street, or any small number of streets, in every working-class district in London, shall be organised into a set of clubs, which are by themselves, or in alliance with those of other neighbourhoods, to carry out, or induce others to carry out, all the reforms—domestic, industrial, educational, provident, or recreative—which the social ideal demands.

At the outset, a true insight into the spirit and methods of the Guild will perhaps be gained most readily by noting that it is an expansion of the family idea of co-operation. In the family all ages and both sexes meet mentally and morally, and do not limit their combination of effort to the attainment of any one special object in life, such as the mere physical comfort, or the health, or the financial convenience, or the intellectual development, or the sympathetic encouragement of one another; but all of these aims are pursued at once, and any one of them may become supreme as occasion demands, and each member receives the kind of help adapted to his present need.

The bad effects of forming societies of working people for any one object alone, however good in itself, seem (because they are indirect) to escape the notice of many would-be philanthropists. Such a society causes its members to magnify out of all proportion that one side of life or culture which it aims to develop. We have in all parts of London the melancholy spectacle of groups of people who are in this way made intensely narrow in their ideal of manhood. We may regard as typical the case of a club for young men in East London, which met twice a week for four years simply for the purpose of boxing. The Cambridge graduate, who organised and counselled this institution, was a man of the highest culture, appreciative of literature, a lover of art, a man filled with devotion to the community, but none of these characteristics did he betray or communicate to the young men he had rallied about him. They only knew him as a man fond of boxing. What to him was the most trifling thing in life became to them the absorbing object of interest, the centre and ground of friendship, the gauge and standard of manly excellence. The leading members of the club were continually tempted to quit amateur efforts and become professional boxers, even at the risk of losing their social status in the club.

Bookish pursuits, also, if followed exclusively, have a narrowing effect upon the members of a club. The same evil ensues if only recreation be the end in view, or any one reform or set of reforms, like that urged by the Anti-Vaccination Society or those proposed by the Social Democratic Federation. The principle of relative proportion in pursuits is a clear one. Boxing must have no more conspicuous place in the club-life than it deserves in a rational system of physical culture; while all bodily exercises together cannot be allowed to usurp time, attention, and enthusiasm, to the exclusion of sympathetic and intellectual occupations. If, in his own judgment, the organiser of the East End club of which I spoke, conceded a pre-eminence of worth to the study of Shakespeare or Darwin, as compared with high efficiency in boxing, then he should have intermingled these diverse interests. But neither should any lover of literature sacrifice the physical culture of the members of his club to the appreciation of the poets, nor should he interest them even in their own completest development to the neglect of the altruistic life. Every club, to be a healthy centre of social development, must also interest itself in the outside world and its needs. Industrial and political movements must claim its attention at the same time that it pays due regard to the physical and mental culture of its members.

In its social reform work the Neighbourhood Guild does not even limit its effort—as is becoming the fashion of the hour—to the rescue of those who have already fallen into vice, crime, or pauperism. Equally would it touch and draw to itself the whole class of self-supporting wage-earners, and not only with the object of preventing them from falling into these worst evils, but also of bringing within their reach the thousand higher advantages which their limited means do not at present allow them individually to attain. The supreme aim which it constantly keeps in view is the completest efficiency of each individual, as a worker for the community, in morals, manners, workmanship, civic virtues and intellectual power, and the fullest possible attainment of social and industrial advantages. Thus it includes the rescue of the fallen, though its preventive work is more conspicuous; and both these are subordinate to its effort to realize ideals of efficiency and culture higher than those now prevailing even among prosperous working men. But in pursuing the loftier aims, it must not be supposed to be quitting the rescue and preventive work; for no hard and fast line can be drawn between the former and these latter. The way to save and prevent is often by educating the intellect, and cultivating the taste of the person in danger or already fallen; and, again, the superior development of one member of a family or of a circle of friends may prove the social salvation of all the rest.

Lest so comprehensive a scheme seem fanciful, let it in the first place be remembered that the Guild may always point to the institution of the family as the tested experiment of a co-operative society pursuing as many aims as there are sides to human life itself. And in the second place, it must be remembered that to do almost all things for one person or a few persons is possible, whereas to do any one thing for everybody might be hopeless. Now any one Neighbourhood Guild for the most part concentrates its efforts upon the comparitively few people living in its immediate vicinity. Let it further be remembered, that while one Guild may reach only 500 people on all sides of their life, 500 Guilds would reach 250,000 people on all sides of their life. And 500 Guilds would not be many, if we consider the number of institutions of any one kind in London, as, for instance, the Board Schools, of which there are over 400. Again, it must be borne in mind that those privileges which no one Guild alone could attain, might easily be reached by the combined efforts of 1,000 Guilds.

A further reason for believing in the practicability of this scheme is the success which has attended the several attempts thus far made to carry it out. The first Guild was started about five years ago in one of the poorest and most crowded quarters of New York City. It has had as great success in the number of members and variety of enterprises undertaken as its house-accommodations and finances would permit. At present it consists of six clubs and a kindergarten, and it has recently been accepted by the newly formed American University Settlement Association as their first settlement and centre of work. Another Guild has been started in Philadelphia, and another in Brooklyn, both of which have taken firm root and are flourishing. Two years and a half ago, a similar institution was started in London. It had its origin in a club consisting of eight working lads, meeting once a week in a private drawing-room. It now consists of five clubs and contains 230 members of all ages, representing less than 100 families. It has reached the limit which its present house-room can accommodate. It meets every evening at Leighton Hall, Leighton Crescent,

Kentish Town, N.W. This building, which contains twenty-four rooms, and stands detached in a garden, besides being the home of the Guild, is also what is called a University Settlement, half of the house being used as a residence by a number of university graduates who devote leisure hours to the work of the Guild.

It is true that some of the most important work which the Guild aspires to do has not yet been undertaken. But the first months and years of such an institution must naturally be devoted to the organisation of its members and the inculcation of its principles into their minds. It is something, however, in two and a half years (to limit our consideration to the Guild in London), to have organised five clubs well, and through them to have founded a circulating library, Sunday afternoon free concerts, Sunday evening lectures, Saturday evening dances for members, a choral society, and fifteen to twenty classes in various branches of technical and literary education, and to have inspired the members of the Guild with the desire to plant new Guilds, and to push forward, as they are doing, at least one specific reform of general interest. To have done so little as this may seem to some readers no very strong credential for inducing the public to assist in the establishment of so wide a scheme as inspires the founders of the Guild. But if one considers the enormous disparity between General Booth's few factories, shelters, homes, and labour intelligence bureau on the one hand, and the vast enterprise he has laid before the public on the other, one must see that the Neighbourhood Guild, as it is, does not fall short of its ideal any more glaringly than does the Salvation Army of its new ambition. Furthermore, the social reform wing of the latter is an undertaking for which the staff of the army have had no training whatever. They are, moreover, according to the frank admission of their leader, fully occupied with another kind of work, which they do not intend to abandon. As General Booth says of his new expedition, " My people will be new to it. We have trained our soldiers in the saving of souls; we have taught them knee-drill; . . . and that will ever continue the main business of their lives. . . . But the new sphere on which we are entering will call for new faculties other than those which have hitherto been cultivated, and for knowledge of a different character. . . . Already our world-wide Salvation work engrosses the energies of every officer we command. With its extension we have the greatest difficulty to keep pace. . . ."* The Neighbourhood Guild, though comparatively small, may at least lay claim to being a body of people who have been trained in the special methods and principles which they now wish to apply on a vastly larger scale. Nor, again, may the actual achievement of the Guild seem so insignificant in comparison with its wider dream of future usefulness, when the sum of money for which it appeals to the public is known to be proportionately small. It asks for only £2,000 a year for ten years, instead of £100,000 to begin with, and £30,000 annually for ever after. For there are good reasons, as I shall show later, for believing that after ten years, with £2,000 a year, Neighbourhood Guilds could be fully self-supporting, and could propagate themselves without aid from the general public.

* "In Darkest England," pp. 283, 284.

III.

LOCALITY IN CITIES AS A FACTOR IN REFORM— ILLUSTRATED IN RELIEF WORK.

THE new principle of organising the social life of all the people in one small district renders practicable many an enterprise which otherwise would be Utopian. One of the least merits of the Guild will be its power, when once it is established, of finding its financial support among those whom it directly benefits. Indeed, the idea of organising the whole social life of neighbourhoods may well be called a vital principle of reform, inasmuch as it gives life to many a worthy undertaking which otherwise languishes from lack of support and enthusiasm. And yet hitherto this principle has scarcely been entertained by reformers.

Dr. Chalmers appreciated better than any one else had ever done, the influence of locality in cities as a charm and attraction to the philanthropic worker, and many have followed out his hints. His principle was that each benevolent lady or gentleman must have a special street or group of houses to visit, and visit regularly; then, affection for the place and the people would lighten the labour and transfuse it with pleasure. He also appreciated more than any one else had done, the vast amount of timely help, which in cases of distress and bereavement is constantly being administered with wisdom and tenderness, in the poorest districts, by the neighbours themselves. And so fully was he impressed with the worth and naturalness of such assistance, that he often waited until the last possible moment, before he would step in to apply aid from a distance—in order to give full chance for the spirit of neighbourly responsibility and service among the people themselves to express itself. But Chalmers' scheme of philanthropy was after all aristocratic. While he would organise his rich parishioners into disciplined bodies of workers, he never seemed to think of developing and lifting out of its spasmodic and intermittent state that instinctive philanthropy to be found among the families of the labouring classes in any one street or house.

It is just this idea, however, which is the root principle of the Neighbourhood Guild. Undirected and unorganised, the instinctive generosity of the working people is inevitably sentimental, fanciful, easily fatigued, and excited only by the most palpable forms of want. The poor as well as the rich need enlightenment in their charity; when awakened to responsibility and instructed, their impulsive kindness becomes a persistent principle of all-round care for one another; and if neighbourhood be linked to neighbourhood, each organised in its own guild, but all united in those efforts which are too comprehensive for any one to undertake alone, the whole life of the metropolis will be raised. And can it be raised in any other way?

If we consider the vast amount of personal attention and time needed, to understand and deal effectively with the case of any one man or family that has fallen into vice, crime, or pauperism, we shall see the impossibility of coping with even these evils alone, unless the helpers be both many and constantly at hand. The Report of the Poor Law Commissioners of 1832 pictures well the difficulties of such efforts, in the following extract from the evidence given before them by the assistant overseer of the Parish of St. George's, Southwark:

"Suppose you go to a man's house as a visitor; you ask, Where is Smith (the pauper)? You see his wife and children, who say they do not know where he is, but that they believe he is gone in search of work. How are you to tell in such a case whether he is at work or not? It could only be by following him in the morning, and you must do that every day, because he may be in work one day and not another. Suppose you have a shoemaker who demands relief of you, and you give it to him on his declaring that he is out of work. You visit his place and find him in work; you say to him, as I have said to one of our paupers, 'Why, Edwards, I thought you had no work?' and he will answer, 'Neither had I any, and I have only got a little job for the day, etc., etc.'"*

This witness before the Commissioners sums up his conclusion in the following manner: "Unless you have a considerable number of

---

* "The Old Poor Law and The New Socialism." By F. C. Montague. Cassell & Co.

men to watch every pauper every day, you are sure to be cheated." Although there is exaggeration here, still one might say that in any neighbourhood formed into a local guild it would be possible to fulfil the demand for many friendly watchers to every person out of work. They would unavoidably be at his heels every night and morning, going and coming from work; they would be in shops and factories throughout the district; they would know where he spent his evenings and how, and would still have time for the pursuit of all the other aims of the guild besides.

But the need of detailed personal supervision over the applicants for work or food, clothing, medicine or shelter, may be best appreciated by considering the criticism of the Charity Organisation Society committee on the plan of giving free dinners to poor Board School children.

The following extract will help us to realize what a multiplicity of remedies is sometimes needed in one family in order to render efficient assistance.

" H—d. Father (aged 33 years), mother (30 years), and three children (six have died). A builder's labourer, earning 20s. to 27s. when in work, but losing a lot of time. Mother getting 6s. a week by washing. She is not a good manager, and the house is untidy. Both out of work at time of inquiry, everything pawned, 10s. 6d. due for rent, and family subsisting on landlady's charity. The eldest girl, who had chest delicacy, was receiving one halfpenny meal a week!

" The Charity Organisation Society provided a letter to the Chest Hospital, cod-liver oil and medicine.

" The mother was out of health and suffering from varicose veins. Good food and an elastic stocking enabled her to continue her work. The father had a bout of rheumatism. He was not in a club, and had to call in the parish doctor. He thinks that an eight hours day would set matters right. But the immediate step seems to be that he should join a club, and that his wife should learn to manage."*

But admitting that the Charity Organisation

---

* First Report of a special Committee of the Charity Organisation Society appointed to consider the best means of dealing with Board School children alleged to be in want of food. Printed by Spottiswoode & Co., 1891, p. 7.

Society principle is right, may not its advocates be blamed for not having gone a step further and devised some practical method of procuring the enormous number of workers which would be required in order to carry out their principle? Must not this abstract theory be joined to some concrete institution which can easily bring it into play, before it can become anything more than idle protest against every philanthropic undertaking? The Neighbourhood Guild, while accepting the abstract principle of detailed attention to every case of indigence, supplements this and renders it practicable by the principle, that every neighbourhood—but especially the poorest—should constitute itself its own Charity Organisation Society. Probably in the case of the family just cited, a dozen neighbouring families knew six months before the Charity Organisation Society stepped in, that the eldest girl had chest delicacy, that the home was untidy, that the mother was suffering from varicose veins, and that the father was not in a club. Now in a Guild, the neighbours would have learned that they must provide a letter to the Chest Hospital, cod-liver oil and medicine for the girl, good food and an elastic stocking for the mother, and by moral suasion must constrain the father to join a club, and must help to find him work.

This special function of gaining insight into the real needs of any family is, of course, fully met by Miss Octavia Hill's system of rent collectors. But in this matter the Guild does not set itself up as a competing system, but rather as a larger plan, comprehending the special methods which Miss Hill has developed. Already the Guild in Kentish Town has applied to the landlord of the worst street in the district to be the rent collector from all the tenants. Miss Hill's method becomes infinitely more powerful for good when joined to the hundred other forces of the Guild, which make for social regeneration. There is also the same objection to be brought against her plan, as against Dr. Chalmers'—that it is aristocratic, that the regenerative work, instead of planting itself among the people themselves, and taking root there, is fed only from the upper classes of society. If for no other reason than this, it must collapse before many years, just as Chalmers' scheme did. Surely the history of the working classes proves that any thorough reform of their social life must rest in a movement from within their own ranks, however much it may need the time and attention of a few men and women of leisure at its inception.

Another superiority of neighbourhood philanthropy over the friendly visitations of ladies who live an hour's distance away, lies in the fact that only neighbours can know without prying! Mere unexpected and unplanned accident will disclose to them what others cannot discover without impertinence. Even the rent-collector coming once a week for a half hour or less on an errand not always agreeable to the tenant, must suffer embarrassment on this score. I know from two years' experience on a Charity Organisation Society committee and from frequent visits to the needy, that a more than Jesuitical tact is required to find out the facts and not be grossly inquisitive. I know that many a family has been suspected by its neighbours, on account of the smiling, would-be vague, inquiries put to them by the Charity Organisation Society's agent. But if the neighbours already know, or can know without offence, why should not they be summoned to relieve as well as to give testimony? Let it not come into any one's mind as an objection that the poor neighbours could not afford to confer material relief of the kind that the "friendly visitor" gives; for neither do the staff of the Charity Organisation Society or of any other charitable institution give the relief out of their own purse. But it has not yet been proved that even the poorest neighbourhood would be unable to look after its own destitute. I believe that it would be able. And if money from the rich were needed, it would be only for intellectual and artistic luxuries.

Then, again, charitable relief is quite free from the tendency to pauperize, only when given by those exposed to poverty. Only the man who can truthfully say to me, "I may be thrown out of work next month, or I may fall ill, and then it will be your turn to help me," can give me food or money and not lower my independence.

✳ But more than by any other circumstance, is the sting taken out of all relief given in the Neighbourhood Guild by the fact that here the assistance is only an incidental and not the main occasion of the organisation. How grim a commentary upon the social life of the poor is it that they unite almost exclusively to procure funeral privileges and sick-money, and help when they are out of work! But how tender and unobtrusive such assistance, where neighbours are already knit together by a thousand high associations in play and song, in pursuit of the intellectual ends of life, in the enjoyment of art, literature, music, conversation, and nature! It is terrible when men draw together only in suffering; whereas those who have laughed and thought together, and joined in ideal aims, can so enter into one another's sorrow as to steal much of its bitterness away. The direct relief of the needy is happily not the prime object of the Neighbourhood Guild.

IV.

CO-OPERATION WITH OTHER REFORM AGENCIES.

THERE is no desire on the part of the Guild to compete with other institutions and organisations, which are carrying on special lines of rescue and preventive work. This constitutes its second main feature as a scheme of social reform. It puts itself into co-operation with other reform movements, thus unifying in itself as many instruments of rescue as General Booth's scheme proposes; but with this difference, that it would not ignore and overlap the good work of others. It will not attempt to start homes for fallen women, but send girls who have erred to homes already established; and if there is not a sufficient number of such institutions, it will use its influence to stir up the association, founded for that special purpose, to the establishment of new homes. So with the men who have just been released from prison; the Guild will secure the co-operation of the

Prisoners' Aid Societies for them. So with other kinds of assistance. It will not establish a bank, but, in preaching thrift, will recommend the Post Office Savings Bank. It, moreover, will urge every man or woman wage-worker to become a member of a trades union, or if none exists, to form one immediately, instructing them as to the value of such combination in keeping up wages and in preventing employers from practising petty injustices. Only such institutions will it attempt to establish as are needed in the particular district, such as there is no likelihood of other agencies establishing, and such as naturally would be an outgrowth of the social life of the Guild. For instance, there would be need in nearly every district for a Neighbourhood Guild Residence Club for young men who do not live with their parents, or who, because of over-crowding, might better be away from home. At the age of twenty it is often best for the son no longer to remain under the somewhat narrow and unimaginative dictation of the father, who is too apt to forget that his son is already a man. Now the moral advantages arising to young men from being in a Guild Residence as compared with being in common lodgings are too evident to need any defence. Equally imperative is the demand for suitable residences for young women who have no home. Also each street needs a co-operative coal-depôt, for which the coals would be bought in August, when prices are lowest, and sold in winter, in small amounts, at the market value, the profit to be used for neighbourhood improvements, or returned to the co-operators, as seems best. Nor is it altogether visionary to hope that, under the influence of the Guild spirit of friendship and reform, neighbours would be induced to undertake a co-operative kitchen, at least during the summer months, when fires would not otherwise be needed in the houses. The food could be delivered hot to the family at the very moment when wanted. The quality of food and of the cooking would be infinitely better. The expense would be less, because of the saving in coal and of that effected by buying the food in large quantities. Such a method of co-operation would not meet with the opposition sure to be raised against any attempt to establish a common dining-room for neighbours. This latter would violate the family sense of privacy. But it must be remembered that while the dining-table is the social as well as the physical centre of the home, the cooking stove is not; and so long as the dining-table remains intact, no removal of other domestic functions to a communistic centre has any tendency to disintegrate the family union. The washing and the cooking may well be relegated to the public wash-house and the Neighbourhood Guild kitchen.

Another institution which every Guild would need, and for which the members of the one in Kentish Town are already sighing and planning, would be a home in the country. Each Guild must have its own country house, that acquaintances, and only acquaintances, may be together during the country holiday. A general notion prevails among the privileged classes of society that working people are not sensitively discriminating in their choice of companions, and do not mind the jostling crowd. But it is not so. Only necessity forces them into toleration of the noisy throngs of Hampstead Heath and the Crystal Palace on a Bank Holiday. Even where habit has dulled their sensitiveness, they need only a few weeks of more refined and friendly comradeship to make them hate the noise and coarseness of large pleasure-seeking crowds. No plan could show less appreciation of the social nature of working people than the proposal to establish a "*Whitechapel*-on-Sea." It is the quiet group of intimate friends which must have its own seaside or country retreat. Besides these, the social life of a fully developed Guild would require a considerable number of large rooms for its circulating library and reading-rooms, for concerts, lectures, plays, committees for a score of purposes, for reading circles, for meetings of each of the clubs, for gymnastics, and for social gatherings of the whole Guild. So little, however, does it wish to compete with other institutions that even education in the ordinary branches would gladly be handed over to polytechnic institutes and Board-School evening classes, since, in the Neighbourhood Guild, education, in the conventional sense of the word, is subordinate to the development of the sympathetic and moral nature of its members, and this development is best reached in the social and business meetings and the committee councils of the various clubs.

I cannot better illustrate the actual relation

of the Guild to other institutions and the kind of reform work it aims at accomplishing immediately, than by quoting Mr. Bosanquet's suggestions as to what the Salvation Army might do, but does not; for it is what the Guild already does, to a certain degree, and hopes to do on a vastly larger scale, as soon as it has made its methods more widely known. Mr. Bosanquet says:* "(1) With such a force as the Army has at command, able to visit thoroughly in all the poorest quarters, they might lay before the Sanitary Authority in every district, from month to month, a complete list of all insanitary dwellings; and they might spirit up the inhabitants to make the necessary complaints, without which it is so very hard to get magistrates to enforce the law. (2) With such a force as the Army has at command, going in and out among the people, and belonging to the same trades and occupations, they might soon by example and precept make it an unknown thing that any man in regular work should not belong to a first-rate, sound Friendly Society, and that any children should not be sent regu-

* See "'In Darkest England' on the Wrong Track," p. 53.

larly to school. Children miss school through change of residence; the Salvation Army might call on all new-comers in the street, and say: "If you really wish to do right, send your children to school, and don't wait for the visitor to find you out." And by doing these simple things they would do higher good, and more of it, and to infinitely more people and in a much shorter time, than a hundred General Booths and a thousand farm colonies could do. But I have never heard that they have made any beginning to do anything whatever of the kind; and therefore I say that they have not yet acquired familiar experience of the actual methods which are most efficient in benefiting the poorer wage-earners.

"The case of the east end bootmaker (Mr. T.),[*] shows the same thing; that case was not stated or treated by a person of experience. I say, then, that the Army has not yet turned its attention to becoming a body of trained workers on secular lines, although I should quite think that the members of the Army are better material for such workers than any other philanthropic organisation has at command. But

[*] *Ibid.* p. 27.

they have gone mad about the creation of a new institution on a large scale, and this is not to be surprised at; it is always the first resort of the inexperienced, because it seems a direct method."

But what the Salvation Army is not, and does not intend to be, yet what Mr. Bosanquet and many wish it might be, the Neighbourhood Guilds is in its very essence, namely : " a body of trained workers on secular lines," turning " its attention to the simple details of local and individual work among the poor."

V.

Neutrality in Religion.

Another prominent characteristic of the Neighbourhood Guild is that it draws together neighbours of all religions and of no religious opinions, and makes of them enthusiastic workers for the good of the community; it only demands unselfishness of conduct. On this basis of neutrality in religion, and with no ulterior motive of religious propaganda, the Neighbourhood Guild worker can enter houses and win the confidence and co-operation of families, where the Salvationist, or even the Churchman sent by the Church, would be met with coldness and suspicion. I have heard a hundred young men and women in the few Guilds already existing say—and even when they themselves were devout Christians: "The reason our Guild succeeds so well is because we never mix up religion with it, and never bother anybody, one way or the other, about religion." Furthermore, I know, by frequent conversation with working people, that the great mass of them have a proud contempt for the Salvation Army. It is therefore questionable whether the Army could do the local secular work which Mr. Bosanquet wishes it might. I cannot refrain from quoting what Mr. Charles Booth, in his "Life and Labour," says of the religious services of the Salvation Army in East London : * "If the student of these matters turns his eyes from those conducting the service to those for whom it is conducted, he sees for the most part blank indifference. Some may 'come to scoff, and stay to pray,' but scoffers are in truth more hopeful than those—and they are the great bulk of every audience of which I have ever made one— who look in to see what is going on; enjoying the hymns, perhaps, but taking the whole service as a diversion. I have said that I do not think the people of East London irreligious in spirit, and also that doctrinal discussion is almost a passion with them; but I do not think the Salvation Army supplies what they want, in either one direction or the other.

* p. 126.

The design of the Army 'to make all men yield, or at least listen,' will be disappointed in East London. On the other hand, they will find recruits there, as elsewhere in England, to swell the comparatively small band of men and women who form the actual Army of General Booth, and who may find their own salvation while seeking vainly to bring salvation to others. Not by this road (if I am right) will religion be brought to the mass of the English people."

If Mr. Charles Booth's judgment be correct, then no thorough reorganisation of the higher life, and through that of the whole life, of the people can be accomplished by the Salvation Army. Now, instead of attempting to draw together from any neighbourhood as workers or captains only those who confess certain evangelical doctrines, the Neighbourhood Guild seeks to draw together first the *best* people of the neighbourhood, the most intelligent, upright, faithful, honest, industrious and public-spirited, whatever their views about the fall of man and the atonement may be; and out of these it expects to form the " remnant " of the righteous who shall save the dissolute, the intemperate, the lazy, the hungry, the neglected. It invites the co-operation of devout worshippers, only expecting that no one shall use the Guild as a means to religious conversion. Just as the Guild leaves each special institution to pursue its own line of activity, so it leaves and expects the Church, through the clergy and ministers and through the services and the Sunday schools, to teach theology and to stir up religious emotions. It will in no wise work against such efforts.

VI.

Enthusiasm for the Guild.

While the Guild is neutral in religion, one of its chief virtues is the enthusiasm and spirit of mutual help and of self-improvement which it fosters. Instead of needing to be urged on to work, the volunteer workers who have helped to organise and counsel the various clubs have rather to be held back from over-taxing their strength out of mere delight in the enterprise. They begin with one evening a week; then they want two; and soon three seem not too many, until the other members of the family protest and succeed in bringing back the enthusiasm into ordinary bounds. A tendency to rob the luxurious home of what seem to the worker superfluous pictures, books, and furniture, for the enrichment of the clubs is a charge not infrequently brought against Neighbourhood Guild workers. Nor do the members themselves fall short in this madness. The young men, after working hard all day, are inclined, if there is anything to be done, to work for their club all night. Five young men of the Guild in London recently worked from midnight until seven in the morning to prepare for an entertainment for the benefit of their library, so as to save the expense of hiring others to do the work; then they went to their day's vocations as usual. This enthusiasm is due in part to the friendship which springs up unawares among the members of the club. One young man insisted last summer that if the Guild had remained closed another month he must surely have died. This spirited attachment to the Guild is in great part due to the method of responsible self-government on which each club is based. In the Neighbourhood Guild, unlike the Salvation Army, there is no such thing as implicit obedience—hence the joy of self-direction. There is rational harmony, unity of will; there is the demand that when any member has promised to do any particular thing he must keep his word; but there is no command from any authority above the united will and character of the club. Only if a state of war were about to arise, would the organiser exercise authority. The outside workers who have thus far assisted by their counsel in each club are equally independent and personally responsible; they know and approve of the spirit and methods of the Guild before they undertake work, and then all the details are left to themselves. It is this independence and responsibility, this voluntary co-operation, which gives breath and breeze, freedom and expansion, to the atmosphere of the Guild.

To illustrate the method of government in a club of young men between the ages of eighteen and twenty-six, I may take the following incident: The young men and young women had chosen to have as their Christmas festivity a fancy dress ball. It had been planned that no one should spend more than half a crown on his costume; but a certain set of more ambitious youths insisted on hiring suits for ten shillings each at the costumier's. I protested that I had never spent ten shillings in my life on one evening's entertainment, and that surely they ought not to do so. Then one of the young men said sarcastically in the meeting of the whole club, "We have often been told that this club is self-governing, and the printed prospectus of the club declares so. But of course that is only upon paper!" I saw that he was right; and I yielded my judgment, saying that they had far better waste ten shillings than that I should treat them like children, and break the principal of the Guild. Fortunately, the calico costumes turned out to be so much fresher and prettier than the hired robes, that the triumph was virtually on the side of economy.

This principle of freedom allied to personal responsibility has stirred up an interest not only in the lighter and merrier objects of the Guild, but also in its earnest purposes.

The members of the Guild in New York show the most tender devotion to any family of the Guild in bereavement, or to any member in time of sickness. Not long ago the father of a family, five children of which were in the Guild, was killed in a lift at the factory where he worked. The jury at the inquest decided, on the testimony of the employers and of workmen who had been bribed, that the man was intoxicated at the time of the accident. By the efforts of the Guild the matter was investigated, with the result that the jury reversed its decision to one of culpable negligence on the part of the employers. The Guild is now suing the firm for damages on behalf of the family. It has also assisted the family in a host of ways, so that even without the father's wages it is again self-supporting. One of the young men of this same Guild not long ago was dangerously ill with typhoid fever. The members procured for him one of the best physicians in the city, while the young women sent him port wine, beef tea, delicacies and flowers, during his illness and convalescence. The Guild, besides, by one evening's entertainment raised £10 for his benefit, so that he began work again after his long illness with very little loss financially. In the same spirit, the young women's club of the Kentish Town Guild gave at the holiday season a Christmas treat at Leighton Hall to sixty very poor children. Each young woman of the Guild—factory workers themselves—made some useful garment for some one poor child. But such a treat was only the beginning of regular work on the part of the young women's club for the little folk of the district. Both the young men and women are anxious to spread the Guild privileges by multiplying the number of Guilds in the poorest streets. More than a score of them have exclaimed to me impatiently, "I do wish we could begin the work in Litcham Street now!" And all that keeps us back from beginning tomorrow is the lack of money to pay for the initial expenses. It is evident, then, that the Neighbourhood Guild, although so radically different in method from the Salvation Army, is marked by an equal enthusiasm for good works.

VII.

THE FAMILY AS THE MORAL UNIT OF SOCIETY.

IN another fundamental and yet quite a different respect the Guild is totally unlike almost every other institution of the People. It regards the family as the true moral unit of society. This it would hold intact, would raise into conformity with its ideal, and make use of as a stronghold of the wider civic virtues. The Guild aims at including all the members of any family; and thus, if there are seven in it, would bring a sevenfold influence for good to bear upon each member—in the first place, directly upon each; and again, indirectly through the six others. This principle is not applied by trades unions, friendly societies, working girls' or working men's clubs, Young Men's or Young Women's Christian Associations, polytechnic institutions or political clubs. All of these, by separating, in their social life, young and old, boys and girls, men and women, Tories and Liberals, or men of different trades and women of different trades, maim and cripple the many-sided humanity of the persons they would benefit.

It is not easy to see how any other institution than the Neighbourhood Guild could hold inviolable the social life of the family, and yet at the same time allure the members into wider associations. But the Guild can do this, and thereby not only strengthens the family tie, but transforms the family from what it almost always is, an exclusive and selfish monopoly of what is best in life, into an agent for fostering and dispensing the highest blessings to the surrounding community. The family finds its truest social function by entering as a family into co-operation with other families for objects beneficial to all.

Since the Guild consists of a group of clubs for all ages and both sexes, each club in it exercises a wholly different moral influence upon its members from what it would if isolated. For instance, although our young woman's club is very similar in its internal management and work to all the ordinary working girls' clubs, no one could make a greater mistake than to classify it with them. For a working girls' club becomes a totally different institution when it is part of a Guild to which belong the father and mother, the brothers and little sisters. The club in the Guild leads the girl in her longing for social pleasures into her family, the working girls' club by itself, on the contrary, leads her away from home friendships. I question whether by itself it ought ever to be established for girls who live with their parents. It is an institution of unquestionable moral worth only in the case of independent girls who live in lodgings. Nor have I any less misgivings as to the ultimate effects of young men's clubs in the Christian Associations when unconnected with clubs for sisters and fathers and mothers. The boy gets a wholly perverted view of sociability, he soon regards it as a relation which only men with men are capable of; and after he marries, he will be so unaccustomed to the idea of comradeship and conversation with women that when he craves social pleasures of an intellectual type he will turn away from home to the political club or even the public-house. I have often visited the large gatherings of young men in the Young Men's Christian Associations, but never without alarm. Where are the sisters and sweethearts and fathers and mothers of these young men ? And why are these men drawn off here by themselves evening after evening? Can there be a doubt that such institutions, in spite of their good intention, are hostile to the social life of the family and to the intellectual and moral companionship of the sexes ?

Yet this unwholesome separation of young and old, of men and women, is not more pernicious to the best life of the community than is the dividing of men in their social life exclusively according to trades. How can class distinction, how can class prejudice and animosity and mutual misunderstanding, ever be done away with if only those of the same handicraft meet together for the wider ends of life ? If about the trades union be gathered the whole intellectual opportunity of the man, then art, literature, recreation, good works and friendship will shed a halo over that particular industrial group, and thus will intensify a thousandfold that very spirit of jealousy already most disadvantageous to the cause of universal labour organisation.

E

The public-house has long been introducing side attractions—splendid lights and carved woodwork, reading-rooms, music, friendly sick-club privileges—in order to meet the new and wider needs of working men; but this adornment of the path that leads to drunkenness is not less seductive than the tendency to make trades' associations the rallying point of a man's whole life. Let trades unions remain restricted to the special object of settling labour disputes justly, but let the man's whole life be guarded by an organisation as broad as life itself. If in one family, one son is a shoemaker and one a shop-keeper and one a clerk, is not this difference of occupation only an additional reason for their associating out of working hours? They would then correct the onesidedness of one another's culture.

And scarcely less pernicious are political clubs, the moment they take upon themselves, as they are inclined to do, the whole management of the social life of their members. They, too, have their reading-rooms, their garden parties and dances, their circulating libraries, their concerts, their general lecture courses. But they introduce a sword of division between men who need each other most. Who so much needs the companionship of a Liberal as a Tory? and who so much the acquaintance of a Tory as a Liberal or a Socialist? What will so effectively break down party fanaticism as an organisation of the social life of the people along non-political lines? And how can neighbours ever come to love one another as neighbours, if their whole life be divided by political differences? How shall children of one mother continue in manhood their early affection, when all these artificial barriers of trade and class and party are thrust in between them? The more urgent is the influence of the Neighbourhood Guild in preserving the family life, because modern industry in its demand for perfect mobility of labour, strikes a blow directly at the home life of working men.

VIII.

Social Meetings for Young Men and Young Women.

A KINDRED principle, which distinguishes the Guild, follows from its being a group of families. Young men and young women meet together in its classes, committees, social entertainments, dances, concerts, lectures, visits to museums, and excursions to the country. The benefit and protection to the character of youths between the ages of fourteen and twenty-five in meeting young women in this manner in the Guild is inestimable. Nothing so diverts the youth's imagination from temptation and from unworthy fancies like chivalrous comradeship with right-minded women. And as each Guild always starts with such, and tends to raise all who enter, up to their standard, it is always a centre of refining influence for men.

But more than this—five years' experience

in the Neighbourhood Guilds confirms the belief that the constant companionship of seventy young men and seventy young women is the surest safeguard against hasty and too early marriage. Of the young men and women in the Forsyth Street Neighbourhood Guild in New York, who have now met evening after evening for nearly five years, not one has married, and only one engagement has been formed, yet many of the members are two-and-twenty and three-and-twenty years old. It is well that every young man and every young woman should know by long acquaintance fifty or a hundred members of the other sex. Then, if they marry from among that number, there is a strong probability of congenial taste and character.

It should be said, further, in order to disarm a common prejudice, that in the Guild there is no promiscuous and unregulated meeting of the young men and women. And especially in the dancing and social evenings is the regulation strict; no one is ever admitted to them except the members of clubs, the same persons who have been meeting week after week for other more serious objects. Those, therefore, who would rightly condemn the bringing in of all sorts of people from the street and the allowing of them to dance together, must recognise in the exclusive nature of the Guild dances a safeguard that is certain to prevent impropriety.

IX.
The Division of a Guild into Clubs.

THE bringing of both sexes and of all ages together in the Guild is not more fundamentally a peculiarity of it than is the subdivision into a number of clubs, separated according to age and sex. The reasons for this division are not far to seek. Boys between the ages of twelve and seventeen have a certain quality of mind in common, which draws them naturally together; and when they are formed into a club, the natural affinity becomes elevated into a manly *esprit de corps*. Also, their tastes being similar, the same occupations interest them. But more than this, the same moral discipline the same instruction in conduct, and the same warnings against error, apply to them all. To illustrate the specific treatment of boys in a club, consider how admirably the study of nature, of birds and crystals and shells, assists in the moral development of youths. An interest in the collection of natural objects is the surest and happiest means of diverting the boy's imagination from a morbid direction, at an age when he is liable to be unduly preoccupied with himself. And in a club the interest in such studies may readily be fanned into an enthusiasm.

Now, with girls, there is not the same reason for the study of natural history. But besides the difference of methods in treatment and instruction, there is also a further reason for distinct clubs for boys and girls. Boys should feel themselves to be men, not simply as individuals, but in common as representatives of a natural class; and girls ought to be made conscious of the common lot of all women and to sympathise with all, as well as to recognise their own lot as individuals. And, furthermore, however much men may care for the society of women, and women for that of men, there is also a distinct and natural liking of men for the society of their own sex, and of women for theirs. Both these attachments should be satisfied, and the Guild meets this need by having separate clubs for each sex and then uniting the clubs for various intellectual and recreative objects. There is also a special advantage to women in having a self-governing club of their own, because there they learn executive management and organisation, and gain practice in speaking, debating and co-operating in practical work; whereas, if women are only in the same club with men, they are certain, with rare exceptions, to stay in the background, while the men come to the front and do all the initiative work. But if boys between twelve and seventeen, and girls between the same ages, form natural groups, so do young men between seventeen and twenty-five, and women of corresponding years. Beyond this limit of age, all men feel themselves on easy and natural terms of conversation with one another, as also do women above twenty-five years old. There is, therefore, a natural division of all persons over twelve years old into six clubs, three for men and boys, and three for women and girls. Yet experience in the Guild work proves that there should not be an advancement of the members of a younger club into an older, for that breaks up the friendships and the moral attachment to the club, but rather must each of the younger clubs each year raise the age of admission for new members; so that the club which now consists of boys will in five years be the young men's club, and so on, while a new club of young boys and girls must be formed every few years for those just leaving school.

Before turning from the subject of the subdivision of the Guild into clubs according to age and sex, I must not omit to refer to the strong spirit of group-emulation which the inevitable comparison of each club with the others of the Guild engenders. It thus appeals to the motive which the early French Socialists believed would be powerful enough, as an incentive to work, to take the place of individual competition. Each club, seeing the excellence of the others, is not satisfied until it has reached the same standard. Especially is the rivalry between young men's and young women's clubs always spirited and wholesome. Neither will allow the other to outdo it in generous support of the Guild, in the quality of its entertainments, in the economic and parliamentary management of its finances and business meetings. It should, however, be noted that, although there is emulation, there is no competition for prizes.

This same principle of emulation would come into play on a large scale if there were a number of connected Guilds. There would spring up a rivalry of one with the other, and a corresponding intensification of interest in every intellectual or social undertaking of the Guild.

X.

The Space Needed for one Guild.

Before the general principles and methods are further elucidated, it may be well to explain certain details of our work, which persons who are interested in the scheme and wish to start on similar lines always ask about.

First, as to the amount of room needed for six clubs. If all the members of each club met together every evening, then six rooms large enough to accommodate them would be needed; but the practice, adopted for other reasons, of not allowing any club to have more than one regular and formal meeting a week enables one large room to serve all the clubs. At Leighton Hall, for example, the largest room, which is 40 feet by 20, is at present used on Monday evenings by the Choral Society, to which members of all the clubs and non-members belong; on Tuesday evenings by the Young Women's Club, for gymnastics and their literary, musical, and business meeting; on Wednesdays by the club of younger boys, who, during one hour of the evening, are joined by the little girls for a dancing class; on Thursday evenings by the young men, for their regular meetings; on Fridays by the older men and women; on Saturdays this same room is used by the young men and women, 140 in all, for dancing and for musical entertainments; on Sunday afternoons, at 4 o'clock, the free concert takes place in it; on Sunday evenings, at 8 o'clock, the free lectures, followed by discussions, are held there. Although it might be thought that this one room did its fair share of work, yet so desirous are the organisers of the Guild to make good use of the space at their disposal, that their conscience will not be freed from a haunting sense of waste until the room is used every Sunday morning for working men's classes, such as have proved successful in many cities in England; every Saturday afternoon, as a play-room for the poorest Board School children of the district; and the rest of the week during the day time as a free model kindergarten, or possibly as a *crèche*. So much might be accomplished by means of one room, if there were attached to it some place for stowing away furniture when not in use.

If other rooms are at the disposal of the Guild, they can be made use of for equally diverse and manifold purposes. One room may be used for several objects and for several sets of persons in one evening. Our library is occupied from six to eight on Wednesdays by the little girls; at eight the carpenter's bench and tools are carried in, and until ten o'clock the room is used by the carpentry class; then a committee may take possession for three-quarters of an hour to plan the wider campaign of the Guild, or, if you please, to dream dreams of a mighty service to mankind. The Guild at Leighton Hall has at its disposal eight rooms altogether: more would be a blessing; it might make shift with less. Spacious apartments for a Guild hold the same relation to its inner life and growth as they do to the social life and aims of a private family—they are no more and no less essential. A Neighbourhood Guild in one room is a Guild "for a' that." Indeed, the one in Kentish Town has been in its present quarters only fourteen months; previously it rented a schoolroom for only two nights a week.

XI.

THE LIMIT OF MEMBERSHIP IN ONE CLUB.

ANOTHER question of detail, involving, however, important psychological principles, is as to the right size for any one club. In the first place, I would say, no club should ever be larger in numbers than would allow of all the members sitting about in a circle in the largest room of the Guild during their social and business meetings. Never should there be any front seats, or, rather, any back seats, in a democratic social club. Nothing better symbolizes the unity and equality of the members, or fosters these sentiments more surely than sitting about in such a circle to transact business and debate social questions in general, and the aims of the Guild in particular. If, therefore, the largest room would accommodate only twenty persons in this manner, no club in that particular Guild should consist of more than twenty persons. Under such circumstances it would be the constant object of the organiser of the clubs to get the twenty best persons in the neighbourhood, thus to make up for defect of quantity by superior quality. But while the size of the room, if small, may determine the limit of numbers in any one club; if the room were very large, another principle comes in to limit the membership. No club should have more members in it than can easily become well acquainted with one another. Every person who enters ought to be able after five weeks in the club to know and be known by all the old members personally and by name, trusting to the ordinary casual meetings to bring the acquaintance about. If the club be too large for that, it defeats its own end. It must be a home where any one's absence is felt and regretted. Nothing draws a person to any place so much as being expected and wanted. Experience shows that after a club has been organised for a year or two it may raise its membership, if it has room, to seventy. But a larger number would certainly destroy the personal intimacy of the members, the club would then become an institution instead of a group of friends, it would be a debating or political society, or a polytechnic or educational centre, but not an expansion of the family idea. And becoming impersonal, it would be a dead thing, not an inspirer to generous cooperation. I have said that after two years a club might increase its numbers to seventy, but even this should be step by step, lest new elements of the wrong kind come in too rapidly to be assimilated, and thereby destroy the character and tone of the club. A club ought never to have more than twenty or thirty members for the first six months. No one person organising it could understand the individuality and talents of a greater number. It is astonishing how persons who have gained valuable experience in the guidance of others in the home, fail to apply their wisdom when they come to deal with people in social clubs. Any parent knows that with five or six sons and daughters to teach and discipline he has his hands quite full, yet he will probably fancy that the larger a club is the better, as if he could influence and instruct and harmonize two hundred strangers. When I read, as I often do, of the marvellous success of some club, and find it given as proof that the club has 1,000 or 1,500 members, then I know that the founders of that club do not mean by success the inner life and spiritual fellowship; for no man has either imaginative insight or time enough to know and cherish with individualized affection 1,000 or 1,500 men. And I know, further, that unless the friendships comprehend the whole club, they only mean so many cliques and factions jarring with one another. Nothing has been more striking in the moral development of the Guild clubs than the way in which the spirit of the whole has broken up, one after another, all narrower divisions. What is still more important to consider is, that small groups of friends may, since they escape inspection, become centres of demoralization, which will corrupt the whole body. The social club, then, must not be so large that the imagination and the sentiment of its members will be unable to comprehend and love it. Experience proves also that clubs for boys and girls cannot wisely be made as large as those for young men and women, for they need more detailed attention, if one is to win their affection, and to clarify and develop their ideas of right and wrong.

What, then, to the philistine mind is an occasion for contempt—the small size of any one Guild—is really its truest merit. For in the highest things men are never reached and saved, they are never made really happy and free, by wholesale. Still, if the Guild scheme should spread so that it could count 500 branches, it might win the applause even of those who estimate the worth of institutions by statistics of outward and visible things.

XII.
A Radiation of Guilds from a Centre.

But if the Guild is to multiply itself, the details of the best method of procedure must be to a certain extent determined upon beforehand. Insuperable difficulties immediately present themselves if we attempt to proceed without a well thought-out plan. For instance, how can the workers now ready to offer their time and training undertake this enterprise, if the next Guild were to be planted three or four miles away from Leighton Hall? Clearly, if the personnel of the Kentish Town Guild is to be of any service, the next branch founded must be in the same district of London, and the third one started at a point in easy walking distance from the second, and so on. In this way a network of such institutions might gradually be stretched all over London. Now it happens, fortunately and designedly, that the members of the Leighton Hall Guild do not live in any one street, or in contiguous streets, but come from throughout Kentish Town, Camden Town, and Gospel Oak. There would, therefore, be a nucleus of workers already living in each locality of the district, who would become the founders of new Guilds. It is accordingly hoped that, if this analysis of the Guild so commend the scheme to the public as to induce them to assist in carrying it out, then, instead of starting—or, at least, in addition to starting—Guilds in their own neighbourhoods, they will lend their support to a radiation of Guilds from Leighton Hall as a centre. For the difficulty of finding volunteer workers able to establish new branches is greater than one might suppose. Six months' work in a branch already founded is the only sure equipment for undertaking the responsibility of a new centre. If the public encourage the plan, a number of friends will go with the writer of these pages to live—as soon as we can procure a suitable residence for a Guild—in Litcham Street, which is only twelve minutes' walk from Leighton Hall. More than a dozen members of the Guild live within three minutes' walk of that street. They would immediately help to form the new Guild, developing the various sides of the work needed to be done there, as soon as the clubs were in order for action. Then we would go to a third neighbourhood, and live there for two or three months, until this centre also began to show an independent character and a capacity to develop itself. In the Parish of St. Pancras, of which Kentish Town is a part, there is a population of more than 246,000 souls; at least ten Guilds should be developed here before we attempt to cross over into the West End, the East and South of London. In these ten Guilds, however, our experience and wisdom would be growing, and the number of efficient and enthusiastic workers continually increasing, so that we could, in more systematic fashion, send out workers to more distant points.

It should be borne in mind as an argument in favour of a radiation of Guilds from a centre, that ten near one another could accomplish by their united effort a hundred times more than the same number scattered throughout London.

XIII.
A Body of Trained Workers on Secular Lines.

But having said so much about the members of the Guild being trained in its methods, I ought to specify the kind of training, and give proof to justify the statement that they are trained. Let us consider so light and frivolous a matter as the work of teaching seventy young men and seventy young women to dance the lancers and to waltz. In order to introduce this refined form of pleasure to the Leighton Hall Guild, it was necessary for me to invite ten or a dozen of my friends, living a long distance away from Kentish Town, to come every Saturday evening for two months to take charge of small classes in waltzing, and of each set of lancers. But now I could find thirty young men and thirty young women in the Guild thoroughly capable and willing to introduce dancing into any number of Guilds we might start in the district. Or consider the teaching of cooking. One of the young men of the Leighton Hall Guild was apprenticed for five years as a cook. He, like others in other departments, contributed his talent to the benefit of the Guild. He has been teaching cookery to a class of twelve young women since last November, half of whom, at least, will be able under his supervision before long to teach the same course, and they are willing to do so. Thus in the next Guild, from the start we should be able to have lessons in cooking every evening in the week, without overtaxing any one volunteer worker. Similarly may instructors be drawn from our classes in wood-carving, short-hand, elocution, gymnastics, and the rest. A more important skill, which also bears more directly upon the main purpose of the Guild, is the ability to act upon committees of all kinds, and to conduct the affairs of a club; for without this skill social reform and organisation cannot go on. It has been most encouraging to note the rapidly advancing self-government, and the corresponding growth of conscious responsibility, which has been made within a year. For example, the treasurer of the young men's club had always until recently delivered over the money collected from the members' fees to an older friend outside the club, as soon as a pound was collected; but suddenly the club awoke to a sense of the indignity of dependence upon some one outside, and of lack of trust in their own treasurer. Since then the treasurer has had entire possession of the club's fees, and his interest in his work has developed tenfold, as seen in the greater attention to its details and in new devices for proving his efficiency to his fellow-members. This treasurer will be the instructor to the inexperienced treasurer of the Litcham Street young men's club in the mysteries of keeping accounts and of collecting dues promptly. There are also in this young men's club half a dozen members, any one of whom could be the right hand man of the new president of any new club, showing him how to keep order and conduct meetings. Besides, through the system of electing officers every three months, there are as many more members who, having served as secretary of the club, can write out admirable minutes of the business transacted. There is also, on the part of nine-tenths of the members of the older clubs, so thorough an understanding of the objects of the Guild, that I could call on as many as I might need—fifteen or twenty—to go from house to house, in any neighbourhood, to explain to the inhabitants the scheme of social reform about to be attempted among them, and to draw them into it.

How the members are being trained also in special lines of reform work is well illustrated in the investigation, which one young man has been making, of the laws concerning the establishment of public wash-houses and baths, and concerning the way to bring pressure to bear upon the vestry so as to influence it to establish a public wash-house in Kentish Town. The district is sorely in need of this great convenience for the poor. The nearest wash-house is more than a mile away. So great and evident is the need, that one philanthropic person has already established a private wash-house in the district; but it is always overcrowded, failing wholly to meet the need. This Guild member, along with others, is now ready, armed with the law, the facts and the arguments, to help in the effort being made by the Guild to arouse local sentiment and move the authorities to their duty in the matter. This sufficiently illustrates what the Guild is doing in certain lines of secular work, and can do in others.

But, undoubtedly, greater mastery of social problems and methods of reform is needed on the part of, at least, a few of the leading members of the Guild than can be acquired in leisure hours by people hard at work in factories all day. Much of the work also demands attention during the day-time by persons devoting all their energy to it. For these reasons it is proposed to draw from among the members a few who have shown most ability and most interest in the Guild work, and enable them to devote all their time to it. In short, I should become their employer, paying them ordinary fair wages for eight hours' work a day, with ordinary promise of advance if they succeed well. These would become immediately the agents of the Guild, to do whatever was needed. Sometimes they would have to spend days together, merely in studying the question of the housing of the poor, or of sanitation, or of co-operative stores for distribution, in relation to the district they were attending to. They would be visitors and lecturers on the Guild scheme; they would establish in each district a labour intelligence bureau; they would bring themselves into touch with all the reform agencies in London—hospitals, homes for women, the prisoners' aid societies, friendly societies, trades unions, the associations for founding trades unions for women, the Society for the Prevention of Cruelty to Children, the philanthropic institutions of the Church; they would be rent collectors and organisers of clubs. The Guild scheme needs two such agents immediately. The first money spent, after meeting the already existing expenses, will be for the wages of such workers. This plan will in no wise destroy the spontaneous and disinterested devotion of such paid members to the clubs to which they already belong; for it is only for the eight hours' work during the daytime that these members would be paid. The evening work would be volunteer, as at present. This distinction would preserve the natural friendly relation between the paid worker and the ordinary member. For those, however, who had a strong liking for such work and ability in it, it would be an added spur to good volunteer work, if they had the outlook open before them of earning a modest livelihood, while, at the same time, doing work for the good of the community. The wages would not be higher than in ordinary trades, so that no one would be allured into work for the Guild by mere love of gain. But the intellectual and moral advantages would surely be a strong attraction to many, as I already know from conversation on the subject with a number of young men and women. They would be developing their minds, increasing their stock of knowledge in all social matters, and reaping the satisfaction of seeing every day the palpable gains in happiness and character which they were bringing to those about them. They would have the outlook of a permanent position in life, for which they would be growing more and more fitly equipped. The Guild scheme once established, no neighbourhood would wish to dispense with the service of such a benefactor. And yet the number of paid workers would be comparatively small. So far as I can picture to my mind the needs of the case, one such worker for each Guild would be enough.

XIV.

The Guild Budget.

In the question of securing trained workers, the ever-recurring one of financial support has again cropped up; for no aspect of the work is more than a fair dream unless a certain amount of money is forthcoming. It will therefore be well, before proceeding to further outlines of method, to consider the details of finance. We make an appeal for £2,000 a year for ten years, as covering the Guild budget, of which the main details are as follows for this year: Leighton Hall has been bought for £750 for fifty-one years, with an annual ground rent of £1. This has been done by borrowing £250, and taking a mortgage of £500 on the property at 5 per cent. interest. The loan and the mortgage ought to be paid off this year. A £100 worth of improvements and fundamental repairs are needed at Leighton Hall before it will be really in a desirable condition for the uses to be made of it. Another £100 will be needed for the proper furnishing of the class rooms and library, and the wages of the care-taker. The wages of two Guild workers for the year would amount to about £156. The rent, furnishing, care-taking, lighting, heating, etc., of a new Guild house would take £250. And Guild house number three would require another £250. These items would leave about £400 for the establishment of a co-operative coal-depôt, and a residence club for young men, and another for young women, for the stocking of our libraries, and similar enterprises, which would easily absorb the small amount at our disposal.

However large the initial expenses may seem, the hope of rendering each club self-supporting in five years from the time of its beginning can easily be shown to be well founded. After they are well organised into clubs, the young men and women and older people always find themselves able to pay threepence a week as regular fees into the Guild. Four clubs of seventy members each thus yield £2 10s. a week, or £130 a year.

The two younger clubs of fifty members each, with a fee of twopence a week, would bring in £43 6s. 8d. in a year. It is also found, by reckoning from what has been done, that any Guild with four older clubs could give a musical and dramatic entertainment once a fortnight (each of the older clubs taking its turn in the management once in two months), and could in this way, even in so small a room as that at Leighton Hall, clear £4 at each entertainment, on a charge of sixpence for tickets. Such a source during twelve months would bring £96 into the coffers of the Guild. Here we have an annual income of £269 6s. 8d., and no Neighbourhood Guild could possibly require more. If it did, many devices, such as garden-parties once a month during the summer, with admission by tickets, at one shilling each, are known to bring in many pounds into local clubs.

XV.

THE TRANSFORMATION OF VARIOUS INSTITUTIONS INTO NEIGHBOURHOOD GUILDS.

THERE is another way in which Guilds may be started without calling upon the Leighton Hall workers, or demanding financial aid from the public, or radiating from the Kentish Town Guild as a centre. Many institutions already exist which may most easily and naturally be transformed into Neighbourhood Guilds. Working men's clubs almost unconsciously—at least, with no fully preconceived plan—find themselves admitting the women of the neighbourhood into some sort of affiliation. The women are allowed one evening a week, or are assigned the use of a reading-room, or are invited and expected to attend Thursday evening lectures and Sunday morning concerts, or they may have books from the circulating library; so that in reality the working *men's* club has become a union of two clubs, one for men and one for women. In the same manner political clubs for men, as I have observed before, tend to widen their object so as to include the whole of social reform; mere politics, except during exciting crises, fall into the background; and general education, recreation, and social pursuits take their place. Indeed, I have been told that, were it not for these attractions, which the political name of the club would not lead a stranger to suspect, such organisations could not keep alive. It should be further stated that the idea of a Neighbourhood Guild, as I have described it, was in great part suggested by the real nature and tendency of many institutions, whose nominal and professed fellowship and aim were much narrower. Such institutions, it seems probable, only require that the fully developed idea which unconsciously they are already following, be presented clearly before them, in order to induce them to place the women's club on complete equality with the men's, to make room for young people's clubs, and to drop the marked emphasis of any one object like party politics for a balanced and harmonized pursuit of all aspects of the social ideal.

Many a working men's club, moreover, languishes because it has not had the wit to develop itself in this direction. Such clubs may be induced by policy and necessity, as an alternative to breaking up, to widen their aim, and to admit women and young people. The co-operation of the women and the young will give moral tone, life and charm to the men's club. It will prove as great an attraction as the sale of spirits now proves, and would increase the receipts of the club as much. Here is a hint for working men's temperance clubs. No wonder they scarcely ever pay, no wonder men need drink as a pastime, when they have ascetically denied themselves the companionship of women and the young.

The members of working girls' clubs also will rejoice at the proposal to give a number of their club rooms for two or three evenings a week to an affiliated club for young men. Indeed, not only the members, but the organisers would in many cases welcome such a change. The ladies who have established the admirable set of prosperous working girls' clubs in New York city, say that a great drawback to the larger success of their movement is due to the fact that they do not reach the brothers and lovers of the girls. There are attractions drawing the girl away from the club-house of an evening, and diverting her attention from the literary and business pursuits. To meet this difficulty, the clubs have certain evenings when they may invite their men acquaintances. But unfortunately, again, the men are shy of coming to a women's institution. Let the young men have equal rights and privileges, so that it shall no longer be merely a girls' club, and the change would not prove simply a benefit to the club itself and to the girls, but to the young men as well. The need for a similar transformation of working lads' institutions into Neighbourhood Guilds is equally evident and is beginning to be consciously felt.

The Neighbourhood Guild idea lends itself also to the solution of a difficult problem in connection with the work of the London Polytechnic Institutions. The vexing question with these has always been how to meet the needs of the social life, and touch the character as well as train the special intellectual faculties of those who attend their classes. Persons who have been acquainted with the Leighton Hall system of clubs, and who know the social needs of the Polytechnics, have said that the incorporation of the Guild idea into the polytechnic system is feasible. The only drawback I can see is, that these institutions are too large and are situated, for the most part, not in the neighbourhoods of the homes of the people who frequent it, but in business localities. Still, each one might be the starting-point for Guilds throughout its own district. The People's Palace has also fallen into confusion in its attempt to reach and build up the social life of its people. Is it not because the effort has not been dominated by the principle of transforming the social groups which spring up naturally, into a network of inter-communicating clubs for the pursuit of all high ends?

There are reasons for questioning whether even Toynbee Hall, in spite of all its good work, will be a permanent force on the side of culture and character, unless it unifies its thousand scattered and wide-reaching efforts, and renders them democratic by adopting its own immediate neighbourhood as its field of work, by setting its own neighbours to manage its enterprises, and by educating them for this through the discipline and experience of Guild club-life. Leighton Hall has sometimes been described as "another Toynbee Hall," and perhaps (except that the work of Leighton Hall is as yet comparatively insignificant) this is as good a description as could be given in three words. During a residence of three months at Toynbee Hall, the founder of the first Neighbourhood Guild had gained many practical suggestions which he incorporated in the Guild. Several of the Guilds also, like Toynbee Hall, are university settlements. Besides this, many details of the Toynbee work are repeated in the Guilds. And still the difference between the latter and the former is fundamental. The men at Toynbee Hall believe in having no method or system, but simply in watching their opportunity to do anything good that turns up, and in learning the condition and mental habits of the people. Now to begin without preconceived plans is the only scientific attitude toward social problems; but that on principle one should continue, after years of practical work and observation, to have no formulated methods and principles, is itself a dogma. I asked a young Oxford graduate some three years ago, what were the principles and aims of the young men's club which he had charge of in Wentworth Street. After some hesitation, he answered, that he did not know that it had any principles or aims. Then I asked what the young men did during the evenings, what their programme was, and how it varied from night to night. He answered, that they had no programme, and all the evenings were the same. The members boxed, smoked, played cards, went and came as they pleased. Nor could the manager of this club see that it was doing any particular good. I would not imply that this is typical of the Toynbee work, but it is typical of their dislike of method and system, or was three, four and five years ago; and they still decry method. But surely, if there is any reason for the existence of a club, it must reveal, to a rational observer, its aims and principles; the practical effort to improve a set of young men must disclose a best way of doing so, and these generalizations from experience might become deductive principles to guide the extension of the work into any new field. What I would maintain is, that any one reflecting over the various unconnected details of the Toynbee Hall movement, will feel that what it needs, is to formulate the principles which its experience suggests, and that these principles will turn out to be those of the Neighbourhood Guild. If this be a correct analysis of the needs of Toynbee Hall, then it is probable that it will gradually develop the main features of the Neighbourhood Guild. It seems already to be doing so. Its clubs are managed more like those of the Guild than formerly. Its reading classes are gradually becoming a more prominent characteristic, and the differences between these and ordinary classes is the personal and social relation of teacher to class and of the members among themselves, which is the feature of the Guild classes. But I am not aware that the branches of its work are as yet being unified and systematised, or put into the hands of the people of Whitechapel.

The social work done by many of the Churches may suggest itself to my readers as very similar to that of the Neighbourhood Guild, and as easily capable of being developed into complete harmony. The main difference between the Guild and the clubs in connection with religious societies is the same as that between it and almost all other clubs as now conducted. These latter are inspired by no far-reaching and definite purpose of social reconstruction. Accordingly they are aimless and confined to details, they have no further object than to keep boys off the street or men out of public-houses, and to teach chess, draughts, or reading. If they would undertake the constant inculcation of social duties, insistence upon the study of the economic and moral problems of the day, and the enlistment of their members into a detailed scheme of reform, their resemblance to the Guild would be something more than in the mere mechanism of club-life. They must transfer their emphasis from details and matters indifferent, to the idea of reforming society. That would be a greater innovation than the mere adoption of the principles of internal organisation. There is nothing, however, either in the structure of the Guild or in its emphasis of civic knowledge and of devotion to the community, that conflicts with the doctrines of the Church ; and its work seems eminently suitable for the laity to undertake. Of course it would all depend on whether this secular work would enlist the enthusiasm of the religious missionary, and whether he would feel inclined to remain silent in the Guild upon matters of religion. The teaching of any religious doctrines is in direct hostility to the idea of neighbourhood organisation. In the Guild in New York, Jews, Freethinkers, Catholics, and Protestants worked harmoniously together. One word, however, of either theological or anti-theological teaching would have driven away from us one element or another. In London the people who are indifferent or hostile to theology are a considerable minority in every neighbourhood. If you wish to draw men together as neighbours, the only practical policy is neutrality in religion. Whether any Church is willing to assume this attitude in its social reform work is for it to decide.

XVI.

The Way to Start a New Guild.

"How would you set to work to organise a new Guild?" is a question often asked me. The answer is, that there are many ways, circumstances determining which is best in any particular case. The problem, however, divides itself into two. The way to start and organise clubs for grown-up people is not the same as that for young people's clubs.

In order to induce the young to come to a Guild it is sometimes only necessary to invite one young man in the neighbourhood, and ask him to invite everybody he knows. Thus the Guild was started in New York with sixty-three members, and no further advertisement was necessary. The little brothers of these formed the second club, the older sisters the third, the little sisters the fourth club, and so on. In case one person cannot bring in members enough, a visit to the factories of the neighbourhood and an invitation to the boys in a five minute speech during their tea hour, will cause a number to turn up at the Guild rooms the next evening. Circulars also may be distributed at every house in the neighbourhood. And if this distribution of hand-bills be accompanied by a personal call and invitation from some of the Guild workers, there is no possibility of not getting the desired number of members for the beginning. When they have once come together, the first thing is to explain briefly what the club will be like, and proceed to the election from among their number of a president, secretary and treasurer, *pro tem*. This done, the whole evening will be taken up with explaining to them how to conduct a business meeting in parliamentary fashion, and training them in making and seconding and putting motions. No sport is so immediately attractive as this kind of business. Nothing so appeals to their sense of dignity and importance. They feel that now they are at last of significance in the community, and this feeling is a basis for most that is good. Such meetings of the club must be continued once every week.

After a month has passed, regular officers and an executive committee may be appointed. But the committee and officers ought never, as is the rule in so many clubs, and as is a necessity in larger ones, to carry out the management without consulting and getting the permission of the whole club in every matter. Only by such a democratic control of the committee by the vote of the members can a vital interest on the part of all be sustained. Only by such control can misunderstandings between committee and club be prevented. Only in this way also can the members receive such an education in debate, in co-operation, in mutual appreciation, in willingness to subordinate one's own whim to the good of the whole, as will prepare them for participation in the wide enterprises of the community at large. Once organised, and holding a meeting once a week, they will plan the whole work and amusement of the club. Shall they form a choral society? what evening can it meet? Shall they have dancing? Shall every member be compelled to attend, at least, one class once a week? How long shall a member be allowed to get in arrear before he is dropped from the club? Shall the fees of members out of work be remitted? What punishment shall be placed upon members who conduct themselves unworthily? These are a few of the thousand and one questions, of vital interest to those discussing them, which from the first will spring up. A body of rules for the club will thus be gradually formulated out of the needs and difficulties which actually present themselves, and out of the common sense and feeling for justice on the part of the members themselves. Often rules are asked for by persons wishing to start similar clubs; but while rules imported from another club might serve as a suggestion, they must not be supposed to do away with the necessity of building up the Guild code of law afresh out of the thought and character of each new club. Vitality and enthusiasm are more important even than order and discipline.

As to which club—that for young men or young women, or boys or girls—should be started first, it seems that it is easier to get the others to come if the young men be the first in the field; for the younger boys look up to them, and the young women are not repelled, whereas the young men are sometimes kept away by pride, if small boys have anticipated them, or if they should seem to follow the lead of girls. But if there were room and plenty of organisers, all clubs might be begun in the same week, and then no question of precedence need arise.

The problem of how to attract the middle-aged people of any district is more difficult. Their habits are settled, their time already is mapped out, their cares weigh heavily upon them. Moreover, if the young people are organised first, their elders shrink from joining the Guild, which, in fact, gets the reputation in the vicinity of being a young people's institution, and parents are shy of associating with their children in intellectual and social pursuits outside the home. But these obstacles can be overcome. Gradually the parents will get into the habit of attending the concerts, lectures, the dramatic entertainments, and debates of the Guild. Still, there are other and greater difficulties. First, what would be the main object of the club for the middle-aged people? What would they do? They are too old, they think, to care for amusements and games, and too out of practice with studies to care to join classes. Evidently some serious object must be set before them, and it must be many-sided, so as to reach all tastes and characters. It was with a sense of these difficulties and needs that the parents of the members of the Leighton Hall Guild were invited to attend a discussion on " The Need for an Ethical Society in Kentish Town." An ethical society, with its comprehensive aim of finding out our social duties and combining to practise them, would touch the serious side of human nature. The local reforms to be introduced in the district would give the people objects to talk about and work for. An ethical society, having no religious or antireligious bias, would repel neither churchman nor secularist. The position of being the oldest members of the Guild would create a responsible interest in the social and intellectual pursuits of the young people, while the earnest purpose of an ethical society would prevent the risk of seeming to be only upon a par with the younger clubs. Eighteen of the parents came forward after the discussion at Leighton Hall, and signed their names to express their desire to form such a society. The number of members has been gradually growing. This society, although scarcely two months old, has undertaken the management of a Sunday evening free lecture course, and has begun plans for several local reforms. It meets twice a month on Friday evenings for discussion of moral problems, and twice to listen to a lecture on some aspect of social or personal duty. It also is to have a social gathering one evening a month. It has, further, decided to open the Guild rooms every Sunday afternoon from four to eight o'clock, for all friends and all the neighbours, as many as care to come. There will be tea at cost charge, and music and recitations; the reading room will be open; for the most part, conversations among small groups of friends will be the attraction. This Society has already appointed a committee of musical friends of the Guild to edit and publish a book of ethical songs, with tunes, for the use of Guilds and board schools, and other meetings of people earnest for social and moral progress. The success of this method of reaching the older people has confirmed the conviction that, after all, this is the best possible basis on which to form them into a club. The name Ethical Society is, of course, of no essential importance, and, like the other clubs, the members could name themselves after their own fancy; but it does describe the nature of the club and its principles better perhaps than any other. A wise difference of proceeding with the older people would seem to be, to found, as described above, a club for men and women together first, and, then, to form a men's section and a women's section for the special pursuits and friendships of each.

XVII.

Reform Work, Class Work.

It has probably become evident before this, how the members of the Guild would occupy themselves evening after evening for years. Still, for the more thorough treatment of this question, and the elucidation of points connected with it but not yet brought out, it will be fitting to consider three classes of occupation,—reform work, class work, and self-entertainment.

Before considering these points, it will be well to answer an objection often brought forward by persons who burn with righteous indignation against the long hours of toil and the hard lot of the working classes. Instead of asking what the people could find to occupy their evenings with in the Guild, they say: "It is a very beautiful scheme, this, of engaging the leisure hours of the poor in class-work, reform work, and entertainments, but the poor have no leisure; and if they have, they are too overworked to use it in such pursuits. Let the good-hearted reformer first devote all his energy to removing the burdens of excessive toil; then would be the time to talk about uniting the people for intellectual and moral ends." In answer to this criticism, I would say two things. First, what I have said before,—that the only road to the emancipation of labourers from excessive toil is by way of intellectual and moral co-operation. Even trades unions were only indirectly and after a time the means of securing industrial advantages to their members. Primarily, as the event proved, they were educational institutions, to those who entered them, in social science and moral co-operation. They trained their members to think and speak and to care for one another. When that was accomplished, the rest followed inevitably. But if that intellectual and moral co-operation was the prime advantage of the trades unions, why should it have been gained unconsciously, and only as the accompaniment of miserable blunders in executive management, and of terrible suffering from untimely strikes? Let the end of social education be undertaken consciously, systematically, and comprehensively. In the second place, it is not generally true that working men have no leisure or are too weary after the day's toil. Many a labourer attributes to each day's work a certain mental torpor when evening comes on, which is due really not to that day's work, but to a habit of mental inactivity, which has been growing upon him for years. Had he begun at the age of seventeen to devote an hour an evening to study or debate, at thirty intellectual pursuits would have been a recreation to him. I am continually astonished at the intellectual vigour of young working men after a long day's toil. It can only be accounted for by the fact that their higher faculties have not been called into action by the routine of the day, and are now fresh and ready for work. Almost all workmen are free from 8 to 11 in the evening, and when their day's labour has not taxed the brain, they need only a few months' effort, and the stimulus of social meeting, to overcome the habit of mental idleness.

Let us return to the occupations which the

Guild finds for its members. As to reform work, I need only remind any one who has ever attempted to serve on any local committee, political, charitable, or educational, of the vast amount of time it takes to do anything in the way of reform, and he will see how the committees of the Guild will have their hands full of work. Even if in the Guild there were no special educational classes, still the members would be kept fully occupied.

And yet class work cannot be wholly handed over to polytechnic institutions or evening schools, much as we should like to do so. Only certain kinds of studies can be as well pursued in a class of strangers or partial strangers as among friends. The elements of education, reading and arithmetic, and industrial work, short-hand, book-keeping, carpentry, sewing, and the like, do not need the social atmosphere of the Guild to foster them. Not so with the study of literature, history, poetry, politics, and all the departments of social science. In these the greatest advantage is derived from the cordial interest of all the members of the class in one another. Such interest permits a readier freedom in the expression of opinions, a quicker understanding of objections raised, an added attraction to the study. Friendship and the pleasure of social converse supplement the mere love of knowledge and acquisition. The interest in the study is sure not to flag so easily as when strangers come together for the same study. The person who takes up such pursuits, by meeting his fellow-students continually in other ways, readily recognises in those about him sympathisers and appreciators of his intellectual merits and interests. Thus he is constantly stimulated to keep up to the standard which others expect him to reach. He finds a hundred more themes for conversation than he would if he were not in a social circle who cared for his favourite subjects. The mental isolation of young men of the working classes, who, having a gift for the higher studies, have carried their education beyond that of their comrades in work and social position, is pathetic. They have no social life on the intellectual plane. A hunger has been awakened in them which only the society of kindred minds could satisfy. Educational institutions have trained them to think and to love to think, but thought can grow clear and sound only by the contact of thinker with thinker. Hence, these people, who have only books and formal instruction, fall into strange and weird conceits. Indeed, no true culture, no true sense of mental perspective, no harmony or proportion in ideas, can come about merely through books or through ordinary school work. A constant daily social atmosphere must supplement all merely systematic and conventional education. What educator has not noticed the difference in the effect of any course of study upon two persons of equal native ability but belonging the one to an illiterate, and the other to a cultivated family? The Guild in its educational work aims at supplying the atmosphere of a cultivated family, as well as attending to the special studies that treat of human relations.

The benefit to the intellectual life which a Guild gradually confers, accrues not more to those who crave it than to those without intellectual aspirations. For this latter class there is no other means of awakening their higher mental life. They need just such friction of mind with mind as the Guild meetings afford. They require also the praise and contempt of friends, to lift them up to the mark and make them ashamed of their ignorance. Many a well-informed person has been led by social pride to seek the information he has gained. This motive at present is scarcely ever felt by members of the working class as an incentive toward better education, because no higher standard is demanded than that which children attain in Board Schools at the age of thirteen.

I may take a very trifling point of culture to illustrate the intellectual stimulus of club-life in the Guild. Teachers of Board Schools take great pains to teach the pupils not to drop their h's and not to prefix them to the wrong words. Often the children learn to speak correctly in this respect during school hours; but the moment they are at home again or playing in the street, they adopt the dialect of the family. In the debates and classes of the Guild, because such errors are pointed out and censured and because correct speech is insisted upon, there has been so marked an advance in the right use of the aspirate within a year, that one could scarcely recognise the speech of certain members as that of the same individuals. So with the grammatical structure of sentences. The members, now, good-naturedly correct one another. A great increase is also observable in the number of words which they use with exact meaning. The regular weekly business and literary meeting of each club also serves as a stimulus to literary studies of all kinds, because it forms an arena of mental contest and exhibition. A youth will commit to memory a poem of Wordsworth or Lowell in order to recite it at the club meeting, whereas he would have no incentive for doing so, were it not for the opportunity given him to display his talent. The six young men who have been taking violin lessons in the Guild for a year and a half, have been held to their task in great part by the expectation of being able to open the meetings of the club with violin music. Our three dramatic classes are inspired for their arduous work solely by the prospect of the entertainments they are preparing for, and of the benefit these will be to the Guild. The wood-carving class has been making panels for one of the Guild rooms. The relation of club-life to educational class work and the way in which each reacts upon and needs the other is thus sufficiently explained. It is clear that much of the time of all the younger people must be engrossed in class work.

XVIII.
Entertainments.

The principle of entertainment by the people, which is prominent in the Guild, is one too often overlooked by the organisers of clubs. The deeper significance of it seems wholly to escape nearly every observer. Because entertainment is merry and a diversion, it is looked upon as a superficial thing, and not serious—not worthy, indeed, to be classed with solemn lectures and discussion on socialism, politics, and morals. But in reality the moral effects of mere merriment, if it be active and self-originated and innocent, are often deeper than those of grim dispute and didactic instruction. Nay, many tendencies to evil can be destroyed only by mirth. Intemperance, and vice, and gloom, and often ill-health, are the special enemies to mankind which the Guild believes it can best help to vanquish, in its own sphere of influence, by the happy spirit of play. It also regards its principle of entertainment by the people themselves, under the moral and refining influences of Guild life, as being the clue to the gradual elevation of the taste of the people, which now revels in the coarse and pitiable inanities of the music hall.

Ordinarily philanthropic workers "get up" entertainments for the people. But the principle of the Guild is to set the people to getting up their own entertainments. And nothing so delights them. The preparation is not inferior as an entertainment to the entertainment itself. Nothing will so make them work and train themselves for a remote issue. Our choral society practises once every week for three months, in order to give a good concert which will pay for music and the salary of the music master; then they set to work again for the next concert with greater fidelity and zeal than before. Our dramatic classes have sometimes worked one evening a week for four or five months on one play. The gymnastic class looks forward in the same manner to giving its exhibition. And there is never a doubt that it is all worth while, because the mere relish of the activity is satisfying in itself. Dancing is a never-failing attraction for almost every Saturday evening in the year. Its being an amusement is recognised as only the fortunate accompaniment of the best mode of cultivating grace of motion, quiet deference of manner, and chivalrous attention to others in little matters. Moreover, whether consciously recognised by the participants or not, all these modes of entertainment are also, as I have said, the happiest means of attacking intemperance. For this vice is one of those evil spirits who come in when the house is discovered to be swept and garnished; often all that is needed is to fill the space.

Now the greater part of the working man's day being filled with drudgery, his evenings ought to be for the most part devoted to recreation. Neither work nor study can on a Saturday night rival the allurement of the public-house and the music hall. He must indeed be lacking in insight who cannot see that the establishment of Saturday evening dances is a most serious and deep-reaching moral reform. Dancing, with good music and bright gas-light, is the only diversion that will attract the coarsest and most illiterate people, and win them away from the haunts of intemperance. And if any one thinks that such amusement, when directed under the conditions prescribed by the Guild clubs, leads to laxity of conduct, I must infer that he is simply ignorant and inexperienced, and does not know what he is saying. He is reasoning from an abstract view of how human nature will express itself, instead of generalizing from ample observation. As with intemperance, so with other vice;—in ninety-nine cases out of a hundred, immorality of this sort would have been prevented in the case of young men, had the imagination during the evening hours of idleness been filled with jollity and merry enterprise. I have known the whole habit of a youth's mind within a few months to change in this respect to one of manly cleanliness, and the whole expression of his countenance, from a hard and repulsive look, to one of moral illumination. But even if these various forms of entertainment by the members themselves did not grapple as they do with intemperance and vice, they would be amply justified for all the time they take, simply because they lighten and enliven weary days and dull monotonous spirits. Harmless pleasure is its own excuse. But because the Guild also inspires to earnest and solemn duties, it has an additional title to its hours of merriment.

The success of the Guild entertainments in competing with music halls is seen in the case of a certain group of young men in the Leighton Hall Guild, who, until they joined it, had been accustomed to attend music halls every Saturday evening; but now, to their own surprise, they have not,—and laughingly boast that they have not,—been inside a music hall for eighteen months. Instead, they have had their own private dances,—where the intervals between waltzes and lancers have been filled with music by Mendelssohn, Beethoven, and Bach, performed by friends of the Guild. The members are conscious of the change of taste that is being brought about in them. As one of them said to me at the close of our eleventh Sunday afternoon free concert, " Well, we shall not be satisfied after this with anything but the very best music and the best performances."

The secret of the way to change the artistic appreciation of people is continuity of training in the better class of art. This principle of continuity, which the university extension movement has applied so assiduously in establishing courses of twelve lectures with classes on any one subject instead of scattered lectures on various subjects, the Guild is attempting to apply to the whole training of the emotions and the will. One high-class concert is as good as wasted upon people who will not hear another for three months or a year, but such a concert heard by the same people once every week for six months will open up to them a new world of beauty and delight. The same principle applies to the improvement of manners. Noisy horseplay and rowdy aggressiveness will not be sensibly softened by one rebuke or by the example of better manners once seen; but at the end of six months, friendly attempts made three and four evenings a week to tone down the loud talking and laughing, and subdue the needless romping, will make themselves felt. Visitors coming to the Guild at intervals of a few months always remark the change for the better in the general deportment. I do not mean for an instant that our Guild members always behave like perfect ladies and gentlemen. Any one coming may at any time note that certain girls are forward and rude, and certain young men ill-bred. All I am maintaining is that the Guild, as an influence, is on the side of refined manners, and that these very persons who misbehave were much worse when they first joined the clubs, and would be much worse now, were it not for the slow but continuous influence of the Guild upon them. When they are in the clubs, there is a probability of their being rebuked and talked with. Even the clubs themselves become the guardian of manners. Only recently the young women's club at Leighton Hall summoned two of their members before the committee on account of rude behaviour, and these two girls have been suspended for four weeks for their misdemeanour.

The application of this principle of continuity in the cultivation of the taste and in the exercise of talents, would revolutionize the amusements of any neighbourhood, which the Guild might have succeeded in organising. If many Guilds were established, it is not a vain fancy to believe that soon the people would have a theatre and an opera of their own. Is it not true that the Guild really embodies what the

People's Palace only appears to embody, namely, Walter Besant's ideal of a Palace of Delight, in which the *people* supply the actors and musicians, and manage their own entertainments?

The great blunder of the People's Palace is its excessive size. If the people are to be their own actors and singers and players upon instruments, then every few hundred people must have their own little stage, and every individual who cares for it have his chance of acting. Those with most talent would soon come to the front. Scarcely any person of genius would remain, as we feel hundreds must now, undiscovered both to the public and to themselves. These tiny Guild theatres would be the training schools from which the most successful performers would pass to the grand stage built by the co-operation of a dozen neighbouring Guilds. If the people's theatre and opera in this way sprang out of the people's best social life, the public and the performers would be keeping pace with each other, the one in appreciation, the other in artistic presentation. And the stage would again become the handmaid, if not of religion, at least, of civic virtue. It would present before the people their own deepest struggles and highest aspirations; it would picture forth the ideals of conduct, character, and society which now haunt the imagination and fire the hearts only of the most gifted poets, painters and prophets. The writers of plays produce whatever they know the people demand. But the people as yet make no distinct demand, they are so crude as to take whatever the financial speculator thinks they would like.

XIX.

The Personality of the Leaders of a Guild.

Having let my fancy carry me to so remote a possibility as a regenerated stage and a true people's theatre, let me turn the reader's attention back to consider that which must be the vitalizing force of the Neighbourhood Guilds, if they are to be centres of higher and broader life,—the personality of the leaders.

It is generally cited as an objection to any movement, that it is dependent upon the peculiar character of those at the head of it. The answer to this should be, that any institution which does not need a strong and high personality to animate it, which can be carried on by a dull, uninterested board of managers or a committee whose heart is not in their work and who have no ideas illuminating their task, is worthless as an instrument for communicating enthusiasm and hope to the people. Nothing but personality can organise the social chaos of the masses into rational and moral co-operation. It is no objection that every Guild is dependent upon the peculiar character of its organiser. It is, moreover, a mistake to imagine that suitable personalities are so rare that, if one goes, no one else would be forthcoming to take his place. At the end of two years the founder of the New York Guild left it in the hands of a fellow-worker, who proved more efficient and original in device than his predecessor. Experience, a generous interest in the work, and the consciousness of personal responsibility, develop the type of personality required. What is more, one Guild is not dominated by one person, but each club has its own responsible adviser, and is penetrated by his or her individuality. In the two Guilds I have been best acquainted with, the most successful clubs were those not under the direct influence of the person who received public credit for the success of the Guilds.

A further fact not to be overlooked is, that the personality of the leader communicates itself to the club, and becoming thus incorporated into a permanent body, acts during the leader's absence. His conscience becomes the common conscience of the club, his enthusiasm burns in them, his wish through affection becomes their will. When absent he is often the more powerfully dominant, for the members then feel a deeper responsibility. A Guild club of young men has been left for three months without its counsellor, and yet has made greater progress during that interval than ever before. I found a touching evidence also of how strong the personal attachment may become, in almost the first words which more than a dozen members of the New York Guild said to me, as soon as I had a private chat with them, upon my return after an absence of two years and a half: "Well," each said to me, "you see I have kept my word, and have worked for the Guild, as I promised you I would, until you came back." I myself had forgotten the half-playful although sincere wish I had expressed so long before; but generous loyalty is not a rare virtue or a weak motive among classes unspoiled by too much worldly ambition. Because of this communication of personality to a permanent organisation like the Guild, the objection that it depends upon the presence of one person is quite unfounded. The New York Guild could, I believe, develop itself henceforward, if left wholly to its own efforts.

But even if the clubs as a whole should not incorporate and perpetuate the leader's character, there will always be certain individual members who are themselves, by nature or grace, radiating centres of moral life. They, when once possessed by the Guild idea and by respect for its workers, will become original and fresh sources of strength to the clubs. A personality of the type needed is perhaps more common among working people than among the more leisured classes. With the latter the conventionalities of society, rather than the opinions and tact of individuals, prescribe conduct; while in each little circle of working people some one man, however bad and unworthy, is apt to be law and gospel. Persons with this gift of influencing others learn to exercise it. Unsophisticated people not only sacrifice themselves out of personal regard, but expect and ask you to sacrifice yourself for them for the same reason. Thus, then, within the Guild itself is found the power that will give vitality to it without fail. Were the Guild ruled from outside, were implicit obedience its method of discipline, then it might not be able to survive the loss of its leaders; but being democratic and voluntary, with a decentralized authority, it will live by means of a diffused personality.

It is thus seen that *personal* work is the very substance of the Guild's activity. And here a common misconception concerning such work must be removed. It is often confounded with *individual* work, with the attempt to deal with each separate person separately. It is also commonly set over against institutional and systematic work. But, as we have just seen, personality may be infused into institutions; nay, institutions are the only means of storing up and preserving it. There is no opposition between the two. Many institutions are, be it granted, soulless, and yet they can hold together for centuries, and work mischief. But on the other hand, strong individual characters die and do no further good, when they have not entered into some state, or Church, or society, or party. We must "make channels for the streams of love, where they may broadly run"; and those institutions are best which give broadest scope to fresh personality. Now, the Neighbourhood Guild is such a channel; next to the family institution, no other gives such free play to character. It is not in danger, as schools and even churches are, of becoming fossilized. Each Guild, like each family, starts with a fresh enthusiasm, and each series of young people forming new clubs, brings the freshness of a new day, as children do to the hearts of their parents.

Before dropping the subject of the personal influence of the leader, it may be well to illustrate the method of managing a club without direct authority. It should first be stated that the organiser never becomes a member, and, therefore, never has the right to vote, neither does he make or second a motion. Accordingly, if no one of the members cared to introduce any measure he might wish to see considered, it would not come before the club. At first a club will seem to have no will of its own and not any power of independent judgment. But, after a year of club-life, the members will have developed a mind of their own. And many a time the organiser will find them voting in opposition to his opinion. How then will he be able to control the club? I should say by superior wisdom and character; or else, in all except cases of downright evil, it would be better that he should be governed by the club. Recently, at my suggestion, one of the young men of the Leighton Hall Guild proposed in their club that the membership be raised from sixty to seventy. But the motion was defeated. The club were quite satisfied with themselves. Why should they take in outsiders, whom they might not care for? Selfish exclusiveness is one of the first-born of the evil brood of pride and privilege, and must be strangled at the beginning. The member who proposed the increase of the size of the club informed me that he would give notice the next week of his intention of introducing the same measure at the following meeting. "But," I said to him, "what arguments have you that will remove the prejudice of the members? You gave no clear and forcible reasons for increasing the number of members. You must work out every argument into minute detail, else you cannot bring the advantages of your proposed change strongly enough before the club to overthrow their preconceived notions." The youth was confused and embarrassed for a moment, for he had not thought out the subject clearly. But a Socratic questioning brought to light three reasons for increasing the size of the club—(1) the regular dues from ten more members would increase the income of the club, and enable it to be more nearly self-supporting; (2) among ten new members there might be a number of fine fellows who would lend their talents to the work of the Guild; and (3) if the Guild be an advantage to its present members, it would prove so to the ten men whom it has room for, but has decided to exclude. When the time came for voting on the proposition, the mover so graphically pictured what the fees of ten more members would purchase, and in what ways the new members could benefit the club and the club benefit them, that his motion was carried unanimously. Let it be observed that the organiser of the club had ruled without obtruding his personality, or constraining the free play of private judgment. This method of reasoning together and waiting until the common consciousness of the members is prepared, before introducing any revolution or reform, is applied even in the clubs of boys and girls between the ages of twelve and sixteen. We are preparing our young people to struggle for political and industrial progress within the bounds of social order.

XX.

Moral and Civic Instruction in the Guild.

Let us here consider the kind of social instruction which the personal influence of the organiser of a club can impress upon the character of the members during their regular weekly meetings. It has long been felt by many educators that the most important branch of knowledge—moral and civic instruction—is almost wholly omitted from the common school curriculum. Children under twelve years of age, when most of them leave school, are too young to appreciate many of the moral and civic problems. Also the mechanical relation of teacher to pupil might destroy the effect of such teaching. But the club meeting lends itself admirably to an older intimate friend of the members for instructing them in whatever details of right conduct they may be ignorant of, and for warning them ; for inspiring them to love the right, for shaming them out of cowardice or hypocrisy or any bad habit, and for encouraging them to fight against besetting faults. The moral influence of the Guild is more like that of home-life than of school. The character of the leader and affection for him give weight to his word, and make civic instruction, not merely an intellectual clearing up, but an emotional quickening. He can reach the will, he can destroy bad habits and build up good ones. He can do this by giving all the minutest reasons for the habit he wishes them to form, and by attaching his approval to the good habit and his moral condemnation to the bad. Take such elementary instruction as that concerning cleanliness of the body. If you wish to induce young men and women who have never been accustomed to the use of a tooth-brush, to purchase and to use daily that article of toilet, it is not sufficient to tell them that one ought to have self-respect enough and regard enough for others to keep the body cleanly. No ordinary person will transform that abstract and general rule into the specific moral commandment: "Thou shalt buy a tooth-brush for 6d. to-morrow, and use it every night and morning!" Yet this is the commandment that must be made to haunt the conscience of nine hundred and ninety-nine out of every thousand of the working people, before they will go and do the thing, and thus begin that levelling upward in trifling habits which will do more than all law and administration to break down the barriers of prejudice between the classes and the masses. The only way to make this special commandment haunt people's imagination is to point out to them the specific evil consequences which neglect of the teeth will bring to health, to beauty, to one's own comfort, and to that of those around. Nay, I have even found it necessary to speak privately to individuals, and make them promise that they will buy a tooth-brush before I see them again; and then, every week or two, if I have reason to think they are neglecting this duty, to plead with them again, and if I have found they have been careful, to show my pleasure and to praise the improvement in their personal appearance. Having given so fully one illustration, it is not necessary for me to illustrate how all other rules of personal cleanliness are inculcated. It must be evident that such a method, and only such a one, can overcome bad habits and form good ones. In the same way as with cleanliness, so right habits in exercise, sleep, eating, ventilation are enjoined and enforced. Likewise with the mental habits,—training of the judgment, the imagination, the sympathies, the temper.

Of the wider social duties and the method of enjoining them in the Guild, it will not be necessary to speak of more than three here, —one in reference to young women, one to young men, and one to parents. The imprudence and folly and ignorance of young working girls concerning marriage is simply terrible. No one has told them of the horrors of wedded life with a drunkard. No one has warned them against falling in love because of superficial charm, against being flattered by gifts of gold ornaments and invitations to theatres. No one has told them what traits of character and what principles of conduct they ought to demand in the man whom they will accept. No one has given to them the view of married life as an intellectual and moral comradeship of the gravest responsibility. No one has explained to them the laws of heredity, so that they would inquire whether

K

the parents and family of the man who proposes to them are addicted to drink, or are affected with maladies that descend from generation to generation. No one has told the girl the necessity of not being familiar with young men, and pictured how one step leads to another, until all may be lost. It is the fashion to attribute the degradation of a large class of women to necessity—to say that the alternative to shame is starvation; but thousands fall where not starvation, but simply plain clothes,—the absence of ostrich feathers and big earrings—form the alternative; and in all these cases the cause is not the wage system, but the equally iniquitous system of letting young women remain ignorant of danger and exposed to temptation. The school cannot give this instruction, nor provide the influence and protection; neither can the home of the poor family. But the Guild can and does give this timely moral information and warning. The lady who has charge of a young women's club will plead with them for prudence, and warn them against danger, as she would if her own sister were wilful and ignorant. More than this, the lady counsellor of the club will point out the necessity that good women shall join together to protect one another. She will bring home the bearing of low wages upon the morality of women, and the effect of trades unions and women's friendly societies in removing occasions to vice.

Equally can young men be guarded against dangers of folly and appetite. There is much talk—which, however, seldom reaches working lads—about purity; but the manly and effective reasons of prudence and justice are seldom given. The dangers of licence, however, may be so presented as to prove an absolute determent with youths who have average intelligence and self-interest, if they are at the same time provided with good companionship and diversions, as in the Guild. And the plea for justice to women, the presentation of the meanness and cowardice of using another human being, and that a woman, to her harm, for one's own momentary pleasure, even though she wishes it, will be sure to purify the character and secure the right conduct of any youth not already given over to evil. But along with these appeals to self-interest and to justice towards women, the

Guild leader will give friendly advice, and will point out the bearing of temperance, health, clean conversation, and mental occupation upon this aspect of conduct. It seems not to be known that throughout the working classes almost the only advice given to lads by men is that chastity in young men is detrimental to health. The Guild leader will make the members see that practically this advice is a lie, and that, even if it were true, it would be no justification for licence, since we constantly recognise that there are many things we must not do, although they might be slightly better for health. The whole of our well-being and that of mankind, he will teach them, is the only test of right conduct. Such is the moral instruction which will be received by the young men who belong to the Neighbourhood Guild, such the guidance that would be brought to the working classes in general, should the Guild spread throughout London. But it must not be supposed that the points of morality mentioned here are made unduly or even eminently prominent in the Guild; there is no tendency in the clubs to dwell morbidly upon these phases of evil. On the

contrary, the principle of the Guild workers
is to divert the mind from this subject as
much as is safe for the members.

As to the moral instruction of parents of the
lowest class, it is ordinarily said, "It is hopeless
to try to do anything for the grown-up people.
Care for the children!" But this despair for
the parents is not well considered. It is true
that many of their habits are hopelessly fixed;
but however ignorant and bad the elders are,
their interest in their children is sincere and
strong, and if they receive enlightenment, they
are sure to take wiser care of the health,
education, and character of their children.
Such instruction, by means of lectures and discussions, can be given in the older people's
clubs. It must be evident, also, that unless
the co-operation and sympathy of mothers and
fathers be enlisted, the difficulty of influencing
children of degraded parentage will be very
great. Here, then, is the special kind of instruction which will have effect upon grown-up
people, if nothing else will; and it is not simply
the lowest class of mothers and fathers who
need it, but throughout society there prevails a
low and worldly standard of parental duty.

No matter how well-to-do the neighbourhood might be, in which a Guild was planted, this phase of social work would not be superfluous.

XXI.

The Moral Discipline of the Guild.

In connection with the civic instruction given in the clubs and the influence exercised by the organiser, mention must be made of the moral discipline exercised by the club itself upon every member. One who had not had experience would scarcely believe what a powerful, and I might say terrible, instrument of punishment a club can bring to bear upon any one of its members. Permanent expulsion may have as baneful an influence upon the character of any delinquent as imprisonment has upon a criminal. It really means, to a great degree, social ostracism. Put out of the club, he is in many cases shut off practically from all respectable companionship. I have known of one young man who sank into the criminal class through defiance of this punishment. On the other hand, I have known others to be spurred on to a new life by the hope of being reinstated in the Guild. The last severity of punishment, unconditional expulsion, we have learned, ought not to be resorted to except in extreme cases. I tremble to think what might have become of certain girls, had they been expelled, as the young women's club of one of the Guilds would have caused them to be, except for a plea for mercy by the counsellor of the club. The categorical imperative never speaks in a more severe and unconditional tone than through the corporate conscience of a young people's club. It is only when they have been trained to moderation, that they do not carry out the extreme rigour of their law. It is only by experience that they learn to apportion punishment to the degree of the malevolent intent of the transgressor, and to the danger to the Guild of letting the culprit go unpunished. Gradually they recognise the difference between suspensions for six, four, or two weeks, with or without formal apology before the committee or before the whole club. The moral discipline of such punishments is increased, naturally, in proportion as it is felt to be mild and just. I have known young men nineteen years old to cry as if their hearts would break, when told that, by vote of their club, they must stay away from the Guild for six months; and upon their return at the end of that time I have known them to show no symptoms of the old faults for which they had been punished. The experience of the Guild goes to show that the strongest motives, if not the highest, that lead to conduct helpful to the community, are the praise and blame of the community as a whole. No less remarkable is the influence of the Guild upon those who wish to enter it than upon those already members; for the former also are constrained by this same motive to conform to its standard.

XXII.

What Classes of People the Guild may Reach.

As to the question often asked, "What class does the Neighbourhood Guild reach?" it must have become clear that there is in its nature nothing to make it inapplicable to every class of society, from the aristocracy down to the very lowest dregs of the slums. All would depend upon the kind of neighbourhood it was in, and the class of people it attempted to draw. In Kentish Town it was deemed desirable that the lowest should not be especially aimed at for the first Guild, in order that it should more easily furnish a corps of workers to assist in the establishment of other Guilds. The young men are plumbers, coal-shovellers, organ and piano factory hands, and builders' labourers, with a sprinkling of skilled mechanics and clerks. They are not what is called "poor people," but are typical of the average honest working class,—the class which the Guild believes will prove the saviours of the unemployed, the idle, and the vicious. Yet they are not well-to-do; they have a hard time of it whenever thrown temporarily out of work; the families live in small houses, and let out rooms to lodgers. Many of the young men repair their own boots.

Morally these young men are temperate, industrious, reverent, and above the average of society, I should think, in personal morality. The young women all work in the various factories of the district, or are dressmakers. They receive five to ten shillings a week, and work ten hours a day; they live at home, and constitute that class which does more harm to women who have to support themselves entirely, than any other; because they sell their labour for what will not pay for their own living, being supported in part by the other members of the family. They are not of the class commonly known as "the factory girl;" that class seems scarcely to exist in Kentish Town. Their dress is good and clean, their face and figure indicate a frail constitution, or at least fine feminine texture. They often faint in the evening because of the hard work in the factory. They are proud and sensitive.

The New York Guild is in the worst district of the city, and a large proportion of the members come from families who know the bitterest poverty, suffering from the drunkenness and violence of a father or mother. Let any one who has access to Jacob Riis's recent book on "How the other Half Lives," read his description of the 10th Ward of New York City, where the Guild is situated, and he will know what class of people it touches and influences. But while the Guild aims at reaching the lowest dregs as well as the lower middle class of society (this latter, also, because of its mental and social poverty, being a fit object of attention), it still does not sentimentally rush directly to the rescue of the fallen. I have often spoken of starting always with the best people of a neighbourhood, and through them reaching the worst. The wisdom and economy of such a scheme must commend itself to every one. In the first place, it ennobles and gives scope to the lives of good people, who have otherwise little chance of benefiting their fellow-men. In the second place, a club that is morally exclusive, immediately begins to raise the mental tone of the lowest neighbours, whereas a club that will take unconditionally all the drunkards and worthless idlers, will repel, and ought to repel, all honest and industrious people. Begin with the best, and the worst will be proud to be allowed to join; begin with the worst, and you will never be able to reach the others. And these others, it must be remembered, although not dissolute and poverty-stricken, do have to lead hard and barren lives, so that they, too, need the privileges of the Guild. They not only need it, but deserve it, and they being of service to others, does not plain justice require the Guild's method?

A distinction, however, must be made between the work of the Guild among its own members, and that among the people of the neighbourhood at large. It is able to reach the very lowest without admitting them into its fellowship. I have already specified how: it is by urging men and women to join friendly societies and trades unions, by securing them hospital privileges, by finding them work, by sending them to inebriate asylums, by educating them generally; in short, by all those means by which the fallen are now being rescued. The Guild would have a number of committees for such work : one for the establishment of free smoking concerts and reading rooms; one for free lectures and discussions; one for the care of the sick; one to act as the poor man's lawyer; one to find work for the unemployed. The ease with which the members of a Guild can find work for any applicant is a fine illustration of the general and unexpected uses to which it can be put. The members need only ask in their respective factories whether any workmen are wanted, and in ordinary states of trade they will be sure to find employment for any one in their neighbourhood. During my two years' acquaintance with the Guild in New York, no member was ever longer than four or five days out of work without having a new situation found for him. It is possible for the committee to put itself into touch with many more employers, and thus extend its efficiency. A hundred guilds with a hundred local labour intelligence bureaus in communication with one another, would solve the problem which one central bureau could not cope with. The Guild, however, while doing much in the direction of individual rescue work, would not attempt to become an employer of labour. Both factories and shelters which are not self-supporting, ultimately aggravate the evil they would cure; or they have no appreciable effect one way or the other, as is the case with them in Germany. Instead of such measures, the Guild recognises as the only cure for a great part of modern poverty and the only solution of the problem of enforced idleness, the abolition of unjust laws which shut out the working classes from their full human rights, and the establishment of new laws to check the evils of unlimited competition and monopoly. The Guild, instead of competing with other employers of labour, would throw its energies into movements for legislative reform. This method could open up new fields for labour in half the time that factories could be built for the manufacture of commodities not demanded in the market.

But questions of legislative reform need not be entered into here. They have been touched upon only to indicate the breadth of action open to the Neighbourhood Guild, and to remove the prejudice which persons impatient for radical political measures, are apt to feel toward any institution, which devotes time and attention to a comprehensive moral and social education of the people. We maintain that the very life and hope of a higher legislative justice, rests upon a more refined and disciplined social intelligence and co-operation on the part of wage-earners.

I have pointed out how the Guild may reach the lowest classes without admitting them into its fellowship. It should be noticed, however, that this fellowship is more alluring to the very poor and neglected than to any other class. The lowest are attracted to a company of people who do not "preach at them," and who do not set up a hundred rigid rules to constrain their deportment and morals, but only invite co-operation in good works. The lowest also discover instantly and like the truly democratic feeling of brotherhood toward them which animates the leaders of the Guild. The English poor, however ignorant, coarse in taste, and degraded by drink, preserve an exquisite delicacy in detecting the faintest tinge of patronage in manner or speech on the part of their would-be benefactors. Many a kind-hearted but underbred person of wealth attributes his failure to win the affection of the poor to their ingratitude, whereas it is due to his own inability to conceal his cloven foot of class pride. The poorest also have the greatest conscious need of the opportunities of amusement, of large rooms, warm fires and bright lights, which the Guild affords.

But its pre-eminent merit, as regards class distinctions, is its ability to break down the foolish prejudice and hatred of each class for the one just below it. When the Guild in Kentish Town was first established, the "junior clerks" who joined it were inclined not to recognise in the street the working lads, whom —rather than forego the loaves and fishes— they were willing to be friends with in the club. I talked to them privately. When one youth protested that his conduct was quite justifiable, that it was beneath him to greet socially in the street a rough working-man with soiled hands and clothes, I found it necessary to inform him that he was quite mistaken in imagining himself to be a gentleman simply because he wore white cuffs and smart neck-ties. I also advised the club to expel any one who presumed to set himself up above any other member. The result is that, since then, there has been no trace of petty class distinction in the Guild, although it includes greater differences of education and wealth than before.

XXIII.

Not a Mere Drop in the Ocean.

NEARLY every reform, if it be of the kind that must begin in a small way and expand gradually by the multiplication of small centres, is continually met at first by the discouraging criticism that it is a mere drop in the ocean. Persons who are accustomed to survey the total sum of injustice and misery in the world, and have not yet submitted their impatient spirit to the humble method of historic evolution, demand reform by one gigantic leap. Such persons would do well to bear in mind the advice contained in the saying: "Enthusiasm only for great things, but *in small things fidelity*." By their contempt for fidelity in small things, many enthusiasts to-day fail of genuine human service, and discourage others from reform work.

It is, moreover, a question whether any

reform can be designated as small when it illustrates a mighty principle, and may be the beginning of a great upward movement. A Neighbourhood Guild seems to me significant, no matter how small it is. Instead of a drop in the ocean, it seems rather to be like a seed in the ground, which, by good chance, may in time clothe acres of waste land with a garment of green.

Nor is it necessary for such an institution to assume gigantic proportions before it can accomplish a great reform. A small number of workers might transform more than one ugly feature of life in modern London into some semblance of the human ideal. Give me only a hundred young men and young women trained and devoting their whole time and talent to such moral and civic instruction among the people of London as I have mentioned above, and I guarantee so to reduce by their efforts the vice, drunkenness, and uncleanliness of the people, that in ten years from now statisticians will have to record a rapid decline in these evils, and assign it to the influence of the hundred teachers of the Neighbourhood Guild.

In conclusion, it should be observed that the

work of organising the mental and moral life of the people about the family and the neighbourhood, although it would bring many immediate satisfactions to the people, would be no mere palliative, reconciling them to the evils of the present industrial system. The hot-headed agitator makes a blunder injurious to his own cause when he advocates the policy of letting things get just as bad as can be, of allowing the logic of unlimited competition to run to its direful extreme, and of granting no present boon to the people, for fear it might lull their newly-awakened spirit back into the old torpor of inactive contentment. Be assured, that the more you give to the people, the more will be demanded of you; whereas, the more they sink under suffering, the less able will they ever be to rise up and challenge their oppressors.

It is, however, illogical to infer, as I have known more than one person to do, that, because the Neighbourhood Guild scheme does not aim at overthrowing the wage-system and the private ownership of land and capital, it is therefore in league with the present order of society, and that its reforms are a mere patchwork of the dominant system. Instead of being regarded as a component part of the social mechanism of to-day, it should rather be classed with those various anticipations, in miniature, of a new order of society—that order which men would still need to create, had the present industrial *régime* been swept away, had land and capital been nationalized, and had the changes proved equal to the hope of the socialists. What else would men do with their leisure hours and increased means of enjoyment than forthwith proceed to the social reconstruction of their mental and moral life, on some such lines as have been indicated in these pages?

Unlike the many utopian dreams of the earlier communism, the scheme I have been proposing does not seek to isolate a group of families from contact with their surrounding society, or to disregard the present conditions and motives of life. On the contrary, it plants itself in the midst of the modern city, believing that in it there is already room to lay at least the foundations of the New and Perfect City.

OPINIONS OF THE PRESS

ON THE

SOCIAL SCIENCE SERIES.

"'The Principles of State Interference' is another of Messrs. Swan Sonnenschein's Series of Handbooks on Scientific Social Subjects. It would be fitting to close our remarks on this little work with a word of commendation of the publishers of so many useful volumes by eminent writers on questions of pressing interest to a large number of the community. We have now received and read a good number of the handbooks which Messrs. Swan Sonnenschein have published in this series, and can speak in the highest terms of them. They are written by men of considerable knowledge of the subjects they have undertaken to discuss; they are concise; they give a fair estimate of the progress which recent discussion has added towards the solution of the pressing social questions of to-day, are well up to date, and are published at a price within the resources of the public to which they are likely to be of the most use."—*Westminster Review*, July, 1891.

"The excellent 'Social Science Series,' which is published at as low a price as to place it within everybody's reach."—*Review of Reviews*.

"A most useful series. . . . This impartial series welcomes both just writers and unjust."—*Manchester Guardian*.

"Concise in treatment, lucid in style and moderate in price, these books can hardly fail to do much towards spreading sound views on economic and social questions."—*Review of the Churches*.

"Convenient, well-printed, and moderately-priced volumes."—*Reynold's Newspaper*.

"There is a certain impartiality about the attractive and well-printed volumes which form the series to which the works noticed in this article belong. There is no editor and no common design beyond a desire to redress those errors and irregularities of society which all the writers, though they may agree in little else, concur in acknowledging and deploring. The system adopted appears to be to select men known to have a claim to speak with more or less authority upon the shortcomings of civilisation, and to allow each to propound the views which commend themselves most strongly to his mind, without reference to the possible flat contradiction which may be forthcoming at the hands of the next contributor."—*Literary World*.

"'The Social Science Series' aims at the illustration of all sides of social and economic truth and error."—*Scotsman*.

SWAN SONNENSCHEIN & CO., LONDON.

SOCIAL SCIENCE SERIES.
SCARLET CLOTH, EACH 2s. 6d.

1. **Work and Wages.** Prof. J. E. THOROLD ROGERS.
 "Nothing that Professor Rogers writes can fail to be of interest to thoughtful people."—*Athenæum.*
2. **Civilisation: its Cause and Cure.** EDWARD CARPENTER.
 "No passing piece of polemics, but a permanent possession."—*Scottish Review.*
3. **Quintessence of Socialism.** Dr. SCHÄFFLE.
 "Precisely the manual needed. Brief, lucid, fair and wise."—*British Weekly.*
4. **Darwinism and Politics.** D. G. RITCHIE, M.A. (Oxon.).
 New Edition, with two additional Essays on HUMAN EVOLUTION.
 "One of the most suggestive books we have met with."—*Literary World.*
5. **Religion of Socialism.** E. BELFORT BAX.
6. **Ethics of Socialism.** E. BELFORT BAX.
 "Mr. Bax is by far the ablest of the English exponents of Socialism."—*Westminster Review.*
7. **The Drink Question.** Dr. KATE MITCHELL.
 "Plenty of interesting matter for reflection.'—*Graphic.*
8. **Promotion of General Happiness.** Prof. M. MACMILLAN.
 "A reasoned account of the most advanced and most enlightened utilitarian doctrine in a clear and readable form."—*Scotsman.*
9. **England's Ideal, &c.** EDWARD CARPENTER.
 "The literary power is unmistakable, their freshness of style, their humour, and their enthusiasm."—*Pall Mall Gazette.*
10. **Socialism in England.** SIDNEY WEBB, LL.B.
 "The best general view of the subject from the modern Socialist side."—*Athenæum.*
11. **Prince Bismarck and State Socialism.** W. H. DAWSON.
 "A succinct, well-digested review of German social and economic legislation since 1870."—*Saturday Review.*
12. **Godwin's Political Justice (On Property).** Edited by H. S. SALT.
 "Shows Godwin at his best; with an interesting and informing introduction."—*Glasgow Herald.*
13. **The Story of the French Revolution.** E. BELFORT BAX.
 "A trustworthy outline."—*Scotsman.*
14. **The Co-Operative Commonwealth.** LAURENCE GRONLUND.
 "An independent exposition of the Socialism of the Marx school."—*Contemporary Review.*
15. **Essays and Addresses.** BERNARD BOSANQUET, M.A. (Oxon.).
 "Ought to be in the hands of every student of the Nineteenth Century spirit."—*Echo.*
 "No one can complain of not being able to understand what Mr. Bosanquet means."—*Pall Mall Gazette.*
16. **Charity Organisation.** C. S. LOCH, Secretary to Charity Organisation Society.
 "A perfect little manual."—*Athenæum.*
 "Deserves a wide circulation."—*Scotsman.*
17. **Thoreau's Anti-Slavery and Reform Papers.** Edited by H. S. SALT.
 "An interesting collection of essays."—*Literary World.*
18. **Self-Help a Hundred Years Ago.** G. J. HOLYOAKE.
 "Will be studied with much benefit by all who are interested in the amelioration of the condition of the poor."—*Morning Post.*
19. **The New York State Reformatory at Elmira.** ALEXANDER WINTER.
 With Preface by HAVELOCK ELLIS.
 "A valuable contribution to the literature of penology."—*Black and White.*

SOCIAL SCIENCE SERIES—(Continued).

20. **Common Sense about Women.**   T. W. HIGGINSON.
"An admirable collection of papers, advocating in the most liberal spirit the emancipation of women."—*Woman's Herald.*

21. **The Unearned Increment.**   W. H. DAWSON.
"A concise but comprehensive volume."—*Echo.*

22. **Our Destiny.**   LAURENCE GRONLUND.
"A very vigorous little book, dealing with the influence of Socialism on morals and religion."—*Daily Chronicle.*

23. **The Working-Class Movement in America.**
Dr. EDWARD and E. MARX AVELING.
"Will give a good idea of the condition of the working classes in America, and of the various organisations which they have formed."—*Scots Leader.*

24. **Luxury.**   Prof. EMILE DE LAVELEYE.
"An eloquent plea on moral and economical grounds for simplicity of life."—*Academy.*

25. **The Land and the Labourers.**   Rev. C. W. STUBBS, M.A.
"This admirable book should be circulated in every village in the country."—*Manchester Guardian.*

26. **The Evolution of Property.**   PAUL LAFARGUE.
"Will prove interesting and profitable to all students of economic history."—*Scotsman.*

27. **Crime and its Causes.**   W. DOUGLAS MORRISON.
"Can hardly fail to suggest to all readers several new and pregnant reflections on the subject."—*Anti-Jacobin.*

28. **Principles of State Interference.**   D. G. RITCHIE, M.A.
"An interesting contribution to the controversy on the functions of the State."—*Glasgow Herald.*

29. **German Socialism and F. Lassalle.**   W. H. DAWSON.
"As a biographical history of German Socialistic movements during this century it may be accepted as complete."—*British Weekly.*

30. **The Purse and the Conscience.**   H. M. THOMPSON, B.A. (Cantab.).
"Shows common sense and fairness in his arguments."—*Scotsman.*

31. **Origin of Property in Land.** FUSTEL DE COULANGES. Edited, with an Introductory Chapter on the English Manor, by Prof. W. J. ASHLEY, M.A.
"His views are clearly stated, and are worth reading."—*Saturday Review.*

32. **The English Republic.** W. J. LINTON. Edited by KINETON PARKES.
"Characterised by that vigorous intellectuality which has marked his long life of literary and artistic activity."—*Glasgow Herald.*

33. **The Co-Operative Movement.**   BEATRICE POTTER.
"Without doubt the ablest and most philosophical analysis of the Co-Operative Movement which has yet been produced."—*Speaker.*

34. **Neighbourhood Guilds.**   Dr. STANTON COIT.
"A most suggestive little book to anyone interested in the social question."—*Pall Mall Gazette.*

35. **Modern Humanists.**   J. M. ROBERTSON.
"Mr. Robertson's style is excellent—nay, even brilliant—and his purely literary criticisms bear the mark of much acumen."—*Times.*

36. **Outlooks from the New Standpoint.**   E. BELFORT BAX.
"Mr. Bax is a very acute and accomplished student of history and economics."—*Daily Chronicle.*

37. **Distributing Co-Operative Societies.** Dr. LUIGI PIZZAMIGLIO. Edited by F. J. SNELL.
"Dr. Pizzamiglio has gathered together and grouped a wide army of facts and statistics, and they speak for themselves."—*Speaker.*

38. **Collectivism and Socialism.** By A. NACQUET. Edited by W. HEAFORD.
"An admirable criticism by a well-known French politician of the New Socialism of Marx and Lassalle."—*Daily Chronicle.*

SOCIAL SCIENCE SERIES—(Continued).

39. **The London Programme.** SIDNEY WEBB, LL.B.
 "Brimful of excellent ideas."—*Anti-Jacobin.*
40. **The Modern State.** PAUL LEROY BEAULIEU.
 "A most interesting book; well worth a place in the library of every social inquirer."—*N. B. Economist.*
41. **The Condition of Labour.** HENRY GEORGE.
 "Written with striking ability, and sure to attract attention."—*Newcastle Chronicle.*
42. **The Revolutionary Spirit preceding the French Revolution.**
 FELIX ROCQUAIN. With a Preface by Professor HUXLEY.
 "The student of the French Revolution will find in it an excellent introduction to the study of that catastrophe."—*Scotsman.*
43. **The Student's Marx.** EDWARD AVELING, D.Sc.
 "One of the most practically useful of any in the Series."—*Glasgow Herald.*
44. **A Short History of Parliament.** B. C. SKOTTOWE, M.A. (Oxon.).
 "Deals very carefully and completely with this side of constitutional history."—*Spectator.*
45. **Poverty: Its Genesis and Edoxus.** J. G. GODARD.
 "He states the problems with great force and clearness."—*N. B. Economist.*
46. **The Trade Policy of Imperial Federation.** MAURICE H. HERVEY.
 "An interesting contribution to the discussion."—*Publishers' Circular.*
47. **The Dawn of Radicalism.** J. BOWLES DALY, LL.D.
 "Forms an admirable picture of an epoch more pregnant, perhaps, with political instruction than any other in the world's history."—*Daily Telegraph.*
48. **The Destitute Alien in Great Britain.** ARNOLD WHITE; MONTAGUE CRACKANTHORPE, Q.C.; W. A. M'ARTHUR, M.P.; W. H. WILKINS, &c.
 "Much valuable information concerning a burning question of the day."—*Times.*
49. **Illegitimacy and the Influence of Seasons on Conduct.**
 ALBERT LEFFINGWELL, M.D.
 "We have not often seen a work based on statistics which is more continuously interesting."—*Westminster Review.*
50. **Commercial Panics of the Nineteenth Century.** H. M. HYNDMAN.
 "One of the best and most permanently useful volumes of the Series."—*Literary Opinion.*
51. **The State and Pensions in Old Age.** J. A. SPENDER and ARTHUR ACLAND, M.P.
 "A careful and cautious examination of the question."—*Times.*
52. **The Fallacy of Saving.** JOHN M. ROBERTSON.
 "A plea for the reorganisation of our social and industrial system."—*Speaker.*
53. **The Irish Peasant.** ANON.
 "A real contribution to the Irish Problem by a close, patient and dispassionate investigator."—*Daily Chronicle.*
54. **The Effects of Machinery on Wages.** Prof. J. S. NICHOLSON.
 "Ably reasoned, clearly stated, impartially written."—*Literary World.*
55. **The Social Horizon.** ANON.
 "A really admirable little book, bright, clear, and unconventional."—*Daily Chronicle.*
56. **Socialism, Utopian and Scientific.** F. ENGELS.
 "The body of the book is still fresh and striking."—*Daily Chronicle.*
57. **Land Nationalisation.** A. R. WALLACE.

DOUBLE VOLUMES, Each 3s. 6d.

1. **Life of Robert Owen.** LLOYD JONES.
 "A worthy record of a life of noble activities."—*Manchester Examiner.*
 "Will be of real value to co-operators, by giving them an insight into the work of one of the most enthusiastic and single-minded of our English Social Reformers."—*Economic Review.*
2. **The Impossibility of Social Democracy: a Second Part of "The Quintessence of Socialism".** Dr. A. SCHÄFFLE.
 "His chief merit consists in seeing that Social Democracy can be best met not by measures of repression but by a constructive policy of social reform."—*Spectator.*
3. **The Condition of the Working Class in England in 1844.** FREDERICK ENGELS.
 "An interesting medium through which to judge of the progress made during nearly half-a-century."—*Pub. Circular.*
4. **The Principles of Social Economy.** YVES GUYOT.
 "An interesting and suggestive work. It is a profound treatise on social economy, and an invaluable collection of facts."—*Spectator.*

www.ingramcontent.com/pod-product-compliance
Lightning Source LLC
Chambersburg PA
CBHW030257170426
43202CB00009B/778